IMAGES
of America

MINOT AIR FORCE BASE

On the Cover: Pictured is *Peace Persuader*, the first Boeing B-52H Stratofortress that landed at Minot Air Force Base, with its crew in front of the aircraft along with former governor of North Dakota William Guy. (Courtesy Minot Air Force Base, 5th Bomb Wing Public Affairs.)

IMAGES
of America

MINOT AIR FORCE BASE

Lt. Col. George A. Larson, USAF (Ret.)

ARCADIA
PUBLISHING

ISBN 978-1-4671-0292-6

Published by Arcadia Publishing
Charleston, South Carolina

Printed in the United States of America

Library of Congress Control Number: 2018955736

For all general information, please contact Arcadia Publishing:
Telephone 843-853-2070
Fax 843-853-0044
E-mail sales@arcadiapublishing.com
For customer service and orders:
Toll-Free 1-888-313-2665

Visit us on the Internet at www.arcadiapublishing.com

This book honors those who served through the Cold War and those who continue to serve in the role of the defense of the United States, maintaining nuclear deterrence and supporting the nation's war on terrorism worldwide.

Contents

ACKNOWLEDGMENTS

I want to thank the entire staff of the 5th Bomb Wing Public Affairs for their assistance in my research on Minot Air Force Base, especially photographs and background material. The 5th Bomb Wing historian provided photographs from his files to look back on the construction of the base. The 91st Missile Wing Public Affairs provided photographs and information on the wing's proud history of Minuteman intercontinental ballistic missiles. The 54th Helicopter Squadron assisted with history about its vital mission to support the 150 widely dispersed missile launch facilities and the 15 launch control support sites, each with an underground launch command center. I want to thank the Air Force Historical Research Agency for information on the 5th Fighter-Interceptor Squadron. Trying to pull documents from the 1950s to the present was not easy, and I appreciate the efforts of "Team Minot" for giving me the material for this book.

INTRODUCTION

Following the Soviet Union's detonation of its first atomic bomb in 1949, US military strategists realized the possible attack route for Soviet long range bombers would be flying out of Arctic staging bases, over the North Pole, through Canadian airspace, and into the northern United States. Department of Defense and US Air Force officials authorized the construction of radar warning stations and military airfields along the US-Canadian border. Previously scarce funds after World War II and the Korean War were approved by Congress for immediate construction.

There was a sense of urgency to protect the United States from a Russian nuclear attack. The fear was being raised that the United States was not prepared to defend against a nuclear bomber attack by the Soviet Union. Members of the Minot Chamber of Commerce worked with North Dakota senator Milton Young to help convince the Air Force to build a fighter-interceptor base at Minot. Minot businessmen and local citizens raised $50,000 to purchase the initial sections of land for the new base. A ground-breaking ceremony was conducted for Minot Air Force Base on July 12, 1955. While Minot businesses wanted an Air Force base near their town, landowners whose property was condemned by the federal government were angry about losing their land and homes when there was no actual declared war. Construction continued from 1955 to 1957.

After the Korean War, the federal government fed into a growing concern among the civilian population of a possible nuclear attack by the Soviet Union against US military installations in large urban areas, including Strategic Air Command bomber and missile bases. Federal government statements noted that if the American people were educated and prepared for a possible attack, they could survive, avoiding death, destruction, and radiation sickness from the nuclear detonations. The Office of Civil Defense provided free diagrams, material lists, and step-by-step instructions on where and how to build a fallout shelter. A separate pamphlet detailed that the shelter should be stocked with food, water, clothing, equipment, medical supplies, and other items to help survive a nuclear war with the Soviet Union.

Unfortunately, during the 1960s, many family fallout shelters were not well designed. The shelters might have blocked radiation, but were not built or equipped properly to hold a family long enough to allow dangerous radiation to drop to a safe level because of the lack of an adequate air exchange system and waste disposal. If a shelter was not fitted with a micro-size air filtration system to block the intake of radiation particles, those inside would come down with radiation sickness and probably die. If a shelter was not large enough to accommodate the number of people inside and lacked proper air filtration and exchange, the internal temperature could rise to unacceptable levels, along with a deadly level of carbon dioxide from those breathing inside the enclosed shelter. Some shelters were equipped with compressed oxygen tanks to add fresh oxygen inside, and even commercial carbon dioxide scrubbers.

Minot Air Force Base was upgraded for the Strategic Air Command with the construction of an alert hangar, control tower, base maintenance hangar, shops, dormitories, mess hall, post exchange, central heating plant, base operations building, infirmary, officers' quarters, security gate, fire station, photo laboratory, organizational hangar, parachute building, pumping station, and 300,000-gallon underground water storage system. Other construction consisted of a non-commissioned officers' club, chapel, gymnasium, and supply and issue building. Work was completed on grading for service roads, walks, ground seeding, parking areas, and fencing; trenching for water, sewer, and storm drains; overhead electric distribution; and an underground fuel storage and distribution system. The runway was of Portland cement concrete, 13,197 feet long and 300 feet wide, stressed to support the combat weight and long enough to allow for safe takeoff for the B-52H Stratofortresses and KC-135A Stratotankers on alert for nuclear deterrence operations.

Minot Air Force Base began operations as an Air Defense Command installation, with its first unit, the 32nd Fighter Group, assigned on February 8, 1957. The 5th Fighter-Interceptor Squadron was equipped with 18 supersonic Convair F-106As to defend North American airspace supported by ground radar and an onsite command center. The Air Force assumed operational control of the base on February 15. The 4136th Strategic Wing became the command element in September 1958, with the 4136th Combat Defense Squadron added on June 1, 1959. The air refueling squadron's first KC-135A Stratotanker, *Miss Minot*, landed at the base on September 23, 1959. The air refueling squadron remained operational on the base until January 1994, when it transferred to Grand Forks Air Force Base, North Dakota.

The construction and operation of Minot Air Force Base helped bring post–Korean War economic prosperity to northwestern North Dakota. Many Minot businesses benefited and grew from purchases made by contractors working on the air base, followed by purchases made by base purchasing agents, along with those of military personnel and their families and local civilian employees on the base. Millions of dollars were pumped into Minot's economy. This was made possible by a relaxation of purchasing regulations by Minot Air Force Base supply personnel to buy goods and services from local Minot sources rather than ordering from central Air Force supply depots. On-base maintenance contracts and construction work provided employment for many of Minot's residents. More money was pumped into Minot's school system to educate military children.

A temporary and exciting part of early Cold War history on Minot Air Force Base was the assignment of a Lockheed U-2 Dragon Lady, a top-secret photo reconnaissance and electronic surveillance detachment to the 4136th Strategic Wing. As part of Operation Crew Flight, the U-2 detachment conducted high-altitude weather reconnaissance flights to collect trace amounts of radioactive debris from atomic detonations. The U-2 detachment arrived at Minot Air Force Base in September 1958. The U-2 came from Detachment 2, 4080th Strategic Reconnaissance Wing, at Laughlin Air Force Base, Texas. Every effort was made to keep the presence of the U-2 at Minot a secret. Minot Air Force Base was an ideal location due to its relatively isolated site north of Minot, its long runway, a hangar to conceal the U-2 during daylight, and launch and recovery at night. The U-2 detachment was scheduled to operate from the air base for nine months but lasted for 18 months.

The 906th Air Refueling Squadron supported the Permanent Tanker Task Force, the Pacific Tanker Task Force, and the European and Alaska Tanker Task Forces, while also flying worldwide tanker missions in 1978 to support US and allied aircraft. The squadron also supported US aerial combat operations in Southeast Asia from 1968 to 1978 and in Southwest Asia from 1990 to 1991.

To support air defense operations, Minot Air Force Station was built 16 miles south of Minot Air Force Base on elevated terrain on the west side of US Highway 83; it was activated on May 20, 1951, became operational in April 1952, and closed in 1978 when it was deemed no longer necessary to support fighter-interceptor squadrons tasked to protect North American airspace. It did remain active as a communications facility from 1978 to 1997. Minot Air Force Station was the first Air Force radar station built, occupied, and operated in North Dakota, prior to the construction and operation of Minot Air Force Base. It was part of the first group of 23 radar stations built by Air Defense Command to detect incoming Soviet bombers and conduct aerial inspection of unidentified aircraft in the northern United States.

To augment the Air Defense Command mission on Minot Air Force Base, the North American Air Defense Command established a semi-automatic ground environment (SAGE) electronic system on the base. A huge, windowless, nuclear blast resistant, reinforced concrete building was constructed to protect the vacuum-tube computers and their operators and maintainers. The building had to have sufficient floor space to hold two 275-ton computers installed by a large team of IBM computer engineers and technicians in 1960. The facility was activated in June 1961. It was responsible for the Minot Air Defense Sector, which comprised North and South Dakota, Montana, Wyoming, Saskatchewan, and part of Manitoba. The Minot Air Force Base's concrete blockhouse processed air surveillance information and transmitted intercept information to assigned Air Defense Command fighter-interceptor squadrons.

The first host unit on Minot Air Force Base was the Air Defense Command's 32nd Air Base Group, activated on February 8, 1957. The 32nd Fighter Group became the first operational unit on the base, joined by the 433rd Fighter-Interceptor Squadron, renamed the 5th Fighter-Interceptor Squadron in January 1958. The first Convair F-106 Delta Dart assigned to the squadron was flown from the Convair aircraft production plant at Palmdale, California.

The 5th Fighter-Interceptor Squadron played a significant role in the Cuban Missile Crisis, from October 14 to 28, 1962, when the United States and the Soviet Union appeared to be on the brink of nuclear war. The squadron maintained four F-106As on the Minot Air Force Base flight line on ready alert inside the four-bay alert hangar at the end of the runway. Pres. John F. Kennedy ordered the four F-106As to redeploy to Fargo International Airport and assume ready-to-launch ground alert. The presidential repositioning order was transmitted to Minot Air Force Base over the secure Air Defense Command hotline. After the command post authenticated the presidential repositioning order, the F-106s took off for Fargo. The deployment was leaked to the Russian embassy in Washington, DC, confirming each F-106A was armed with two nuclear-warhead Genie air-to-air missiles to shoot down Russian bombers. The order also deployed 20 ground crew personnel to Fargo International Airport. Interestingly, Russian Politburo members wrote about this deployment years after the Cold War ended, indicating that the Soviet Union was not going to launch bombers against the United States due to the Air Defense Command's fighter-interceptor deployments; the threat of missile launches was averted due to the fear of nuclear destruction of their country.

The Strategic Air Command equipped the 4136th Strategic Wing with the final version of the Stratofortress, the B-52H, in 1961 as a nuclear deterrence bomber, maintaining a 15-minute nuclear alert warning launch. The base invited Minot residents to see the first B-52H land at Minot on Peace Persuader Day, July 16, 1961. As the Strategic Air Command reorganized its nuclear bomber force, the wing was redesignated the 450th Bomb Wing on February 1, 1963. On July 25, 1963, it was redesignated the 5th Bomb Wing.

During February and March 2003, part of the 5th Bomb Wing deployed to the 4157th Air Expeditionary Wing operating at Royal Air Force Fairford, England, for preparations to strike targets in Iraq. During Operation Freedom, the expeditionary wing dropped 3.2 million pounds of general-purpose bombs on Iraqi targets. For the 5th Bomb Wing, deployments became an operational norm in 2004. The wing participated in the nation's military repositioning to the Pacific in response to increased Chinese military expansion and the growing nuclear threat from North Korea.

From August 16 to 21, 2011, a 5th Bomb Wing B-52H aircrew completed a historic flight from Minot Air Force Base over the geographic North Pole en route to the Moscow International Air and Space Aviation Salon. Russian air force officers inspecting the B-52H were amazed to hear that the US Air Force programmed the Air Force Global Strike Command's Stratofortresses to remain in its active inventory to 2040 and possibly beyond.

During the Cold War, Minot Air Force Base, unlike other Air Force bases that initially used World War II buildings, was constructed from the ground up as a new base using 1950s technology. Its entire structure was intended to support the Cold War nuclear deterrence mission against the Soviet Union.

The 54th Helicopter Squadron is a small but important flying organization on Minot Air Force Base. Its mission is to ensure the integrity of the 91st Missile Wing's nuclear deterrence by providing immediate, flexible, and effective combat helicopter support anywhere, anytime, and on time. A typical flight carries a pilot, copilot, flight engineer, and a two- to four-person tactical response team or Security Forces team. The UH-1N is equipped with forward-looking infrared radar and high-tech camera optics with night vision and thermal capabilities to scan surrounding terrain day or night. It flies in all weather, which can be severe in North Dakota, especially during the winter months.

The strategic location of Minot Air Force Base, 75 miles from the geographic center of North America, led the Department of Defense to locate a Minuteman missile wing there. Initial field construction began in January 1961 and was completed by 1963. The Minuteman I was replaced by the improved Minuteman III in 1971; the Minuteman III remains operational today. The 91st Strategic Missile Wing was redesignated as the 91st Missile Wing on October 1, 1997. The wing's mission is to defend the United States with safe, secure intercontinental ballistic missiles ready to immediately deliver a nuclear warhead on target. The wing also ensures that its specialized security forces are trained, organized, and equipped to protect the 150 Minuteman III launch facilities and 15 missile alert facilities in a geographical area comprising 8,500 square miles. This is a large and important mission to protect one third of the Air Force Global Strike Command's ground-based missile deterrence.

Minot Air Force Base was part of a historic event at all three Air Force Global Strike Command missile wings when all female missile launch officers were on alert in the launch control centers on March 21, 2016. Minot Air Force Base also participated in an all-female B-52H aircrew training mission along with Barksdale Air Force Base, Louisiana.

On August 19, 2015, recognizing the importance of Air Force Global Strike Command's ground-based nuclear force, a 91st Missile Wing Minuteman III was pulled from its silo, transported to Vandenberg Air Force Base, and launched by one of the wing's missile alert crews. The test re-entry vehicle impacted its designated target area 4,200 miles away in the Pacific Ocean near the Kwajalein Atoll. This demonstrated that the Minuteman III, despite its age, is a viable weapon system. But in 2015, the Congressional Budget Office announced that to upgrade and maintain the Minuteman III system will cost an estimated $348 billion over the next 10 years.

Minot Air Force Base started as a Strategic Air Command base hosting B-52H bombers and Minuteman intercontinental ballistic missiles. It maintained a nuclear shield for the United States when the Soviet Union was the primary threat during the Cold War. Today, Minot continues this mission against new, emerging nuclear threats. The wing is also heavily involved in the War on Terror, with frequent deployments to Southwest Asia.

One

Construction and Modernization July 12, 1955–February 7, 1957

The establishment of an Air Force base at Minot, North Dakota, was based on growing Cold War fears of a nuclear attack on the United States by the Soviet Union. Minot Chamber of Commerce officials and Sen. Milton Young provided information to the Department of Defense that, as air base sites were reviewed and constructed in the northern United States in the early 1950s in response to the Korean War and the growing concern over a war with the Soviet Union, Minot was an ideal location for a base. Funds were pouring into the Department of Defense for base construction, and Minot was selected. As during World War II, this required the condemnation of land for construction due to resistance of landowners who argued that they should not lose their land, homes, and income when the United States was not at war.

Construction plans had to be changed from a single Air Defense Command installation with fighter-interceptors to include Strategic Air Command B-52H bombers and KC-135A Stratotankers. The single runway was expanded from 8,100 feet long and 150 feet wide to 13,197 feet long and 300 feet wide, with increased concrete thickness to support bomber and tanker operations. With additional facilities, construction cost reached $20,730,996. This pumped millions of dollars into the Minot economy. The 32nd Fighter Group was the first active Air Force flying unit on the base. Construction was revamped to include a storage area for nuclear weapons, separate alert facilities, fuel storage, dormitories, and everything needed to conduct air defense and nuclear deterrence.

The public was invited to the base's first Armed Forces Day celebration on May 17, 1959, with attendance of over 30,000. Locals had the opportunity to see the completed progress on the base. In 2016, the Air Force estimated that the economic impact of Minot Air Force Base on the city of Minot was approximately $750 million.

Pictured is the original Minot Chamber of Commerce building in downtown Minot, North Dakota, around 1956–1957. The chamber of commerce was heavily involved in obtaining an Air Force base in Minot. (Courtesy Minot Chamber of Commerce.)

Sen. Milton Young, who represented North Dakota from 1945 to 1981, lobbied the Department of Defense and the Air Force to build Air Force bases at Minot and Fargo. (Courtesy US Senate archives via the Washington, DC, office of Sen. John Thune.)

This photograph shows Main Street in Minot in the late 1950s. The construction of Minot Air Force Base pumped millions of dollars into the city's businesses, and after it became operational, the base continued to have the largest economic impact on the city. (Courtesy Minot Air Force Base, 5th Bomb Wing Public Affairs.)

The Minot Airport was dedicated on July 23, 1923. A Ford Tri-motor passenger airplane is visible at center during a 1930 airshow. To the right is a small aircraft, and vintage motor cars are parked on the grass field. (Author's collection.)

During World War II, the Minot Airport was used as an alternate runway for transiting military aircraft. This is a post–World War II photograph, when Minot was a civilian airport. (Courtesy Minot Public Library.)

This maze of metal roof trusses is for the hangars on the base. They were assembled on the ground, raised by the crane in the background, positioned on the walls of the hangars, secured in place, and roofed. (Courtesy Minot Air Force Base, 5th Bomb Wing Historian.)

Pictured here is the first control tower built at Minot Air Force Base for Air Defense Command fighter-interceptor operations. (Courtesy Minot Air Force Base, 5th Bomb Public Affairs.)

This wooden single-story building was used as a contractor's office during construction of Minot Air Force Base. Later, it was purchased and moved off base. (Courtesy Minot Air Force Base, 5th Bomb Public Affairs.)

A bulldozer pushes an earth scraper during runway construction. A 5th Fighter-Interceptor Squadron F-106A is flying low over the base. (Courtesy Minot Air Force Base, 5th Bomb Wing Public Affairs.)

A bulldozer pulls an earth leveler with a conveyor belt loading dirt into an earth mover to remove high spots and fill in low spots during runway construction. This equipment is small compared to current heavy-duty earth-moving equipment. (Courtesy Minot Air Force Base, 5th Bomb Wing Public Affairs.)

A heavy tractor pulls the earth scraper at slow speed, picking up dirt to level the runway and fill a wheeled tractor pulling a large side-dump earth-moving wagon. (Courtesy Minot Air Force Base, 5th Bomb Wing Public Affairs.)

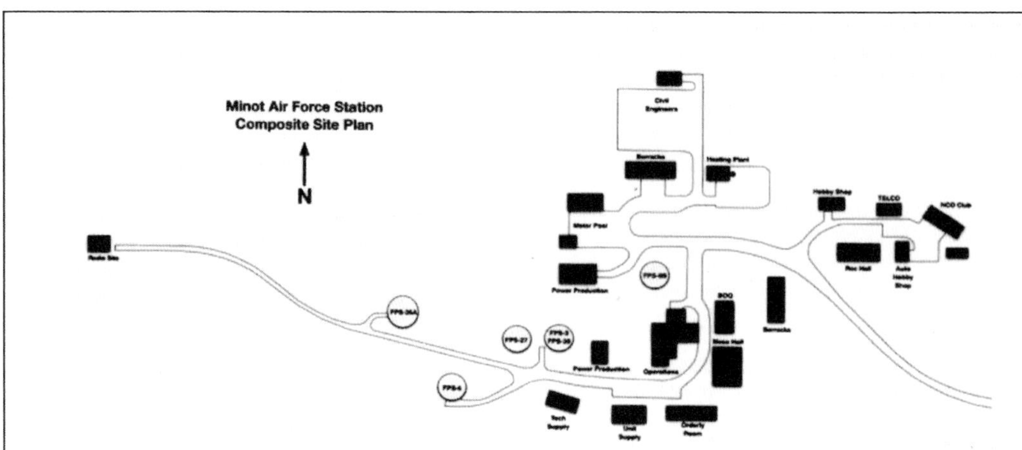

This map of buildings under construction on the base was made to assist in delivery of building materials to the proper locations to speed completion. (Courtesy Minot Air Force Base, 5th Bomb Wing Public Affairs.)

Two large aircraft parking ramps are being built off the main aircraft parking ramp, with concrete being laid. One hangar is under construction at right, and to the left, another is in the early stages of construction. (Courtesy Minot Air Force Base, 5th Bomb Wing Public Affairs.)

A military parking area is pictured around 1961; construction was completed in 1957. The two large hangars shown previously under construction are now finished. (Courtesy Minot Air Force Base, 5th Bomb Wing Public Affairs.)

The foundations are poured for Wherry-type on-base housing, which during the 1950s was the standard accompanied housing for officers and enlisted personnel. (Courtesy Minot Air Force Base, 5th Bomb Wing Public Affairs.)

Shown is one section of accompanied personnel on-base housing, which was built to existing civilian housing standards with attached garages, central heating and air-conditioning, and appliances. (Courtesy Minot Air Force Base, 5th Bomb Wing Public Affairs.)

Demolition of this three-story concrete dormitory, built in 1955, began on July 27, 2010. To the left is a two-story 1955 dormitory that remains operational. (Courtesy Minot Air Force Base, 5th Bomb Wing Public Affairs.)

New construction in 2014 added a large hangar that can hold two B-52H bombers. The maintenance hangar supplements the two B-52H hangars built in the 1950s. (Courtesy Minot Air Force Base, 5th Bomb Wing Public Affairs.)

After initial construction was completed on Minot Air Force Base, the Minot Gate (sometimes referred to as the South Gate) transitioned from a small, wood-framed security guard building to a concrete structure. (Courtesy Minot Air Force Base, 5th Bomb Wing Public Affairs.)

The Minot Gate has steel posts sunk into the ground to force vehicles entering the base to slowly weave toward the gate at a speed of 15 miles per hour or less and stop for an identification check and electronic confirmation of military identification cards. (Author's collection.)

Barracks like this one for unaccompanied enlisted personnel were constructed in the mid-1970s. These barracks improved the quality of life for airmen on the base. (Author's collection.)

B-52Hs of the 5th Bomb Wing require large volumes of aviation fuel, which is stored in numerous flight-line fuel storage tanks like this one feeding into flight-line distribution systems upgraded to support the wing's bombers. (Author's collection.)

This ground-level view shows one of the former Air Defense Command two-bay alert hangars. The hangar doors are secured in the closed position, with access into the building provided by garage-type doors. These buildings are used for storage and other support functions. (Author's collection.)

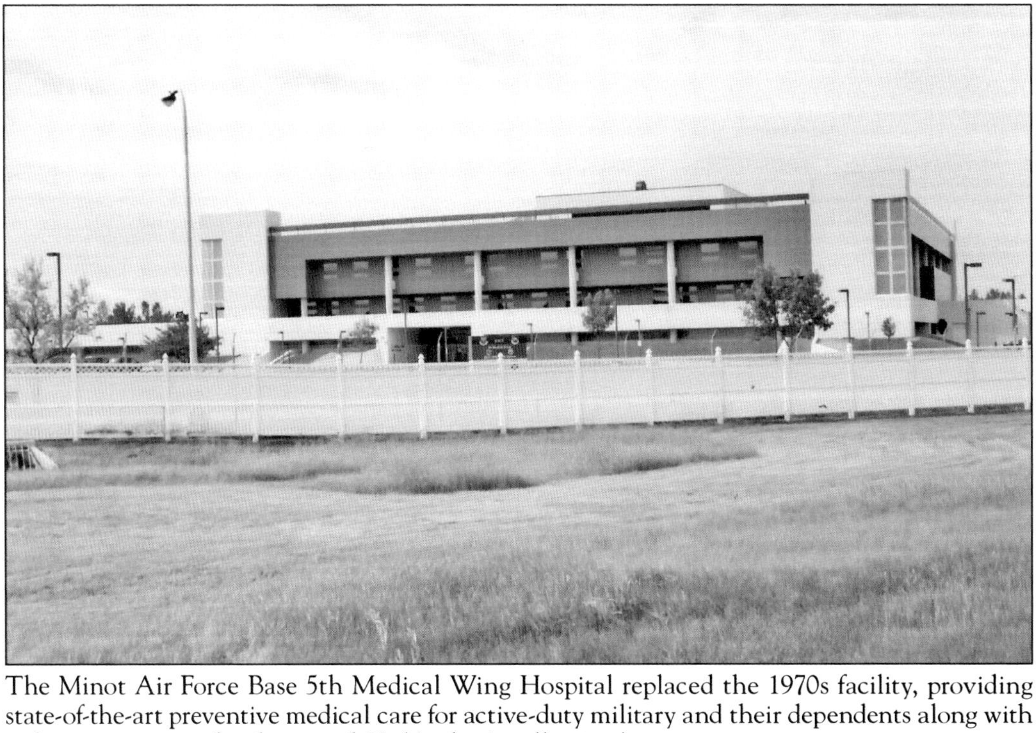

The Minot Air Force Base 5th Medical Wing Hospital replaced the 1970s facility, providing state-of-the-art preventive medical care for active-duty military and their dependents along with military retirees under the age of 65. (Author's collection.)

A large, multi-bay fire station provides emergency fire response for aircraft accidents and on-base structural fires. Minot Air Force Base also provides fire response services if requested by the City of Minot. (Author's collection.)

Pictured is one of the hangars built for the Air Defense Command and, later, Strategic Air Command, now used as a storage facility. The hangar doors are secured in place with access through garage-type doors. (Author's collection.)

Pictured are two of Minot Air Force Base's water towers, which provide water used daily on the base and maintain adequate water pressure to hydrants for fire suppression. (Author's collection.)

This original steel tower had a rotating light beacon on top to provide general night and bad-weather location of the base. The light beacon was removed and replaced with state-of-the-art digital electronic transmitters to direct aircraft to the base. (Author's collection.)

The 1956-era rotating light beacon was removed from Minot Air Force Base's steel tower and donated to the Dakota Territory Air Museum, located adjacent to the Minot International Airport, where it was restored as part of the 1950s history of Minot Air Force Base. (Author's collection.)

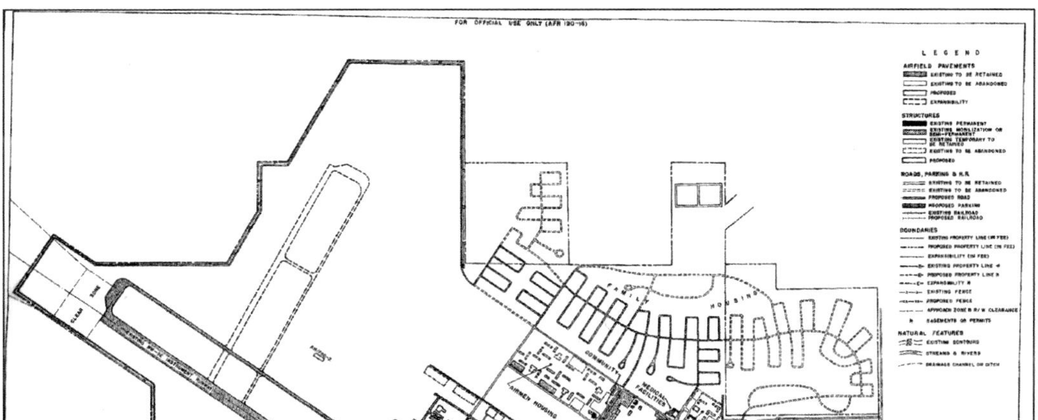

This general layout plan of Minot Air Force Base is used by base departments to locate work areas, with the rectangles marking high-security areas. (Courtesy Minot Air Force Base, 5th Bomb Wing Public Affairs.)

This c. 1992 aerial photograph of Minot Air Force Base was taken from nearly the same angle as the layout plan on the previous page. The wing's B-52Hs are not on alert, due to Pres. George Bush's stand-down of the US nuclear bomber force. (Courtesy Minot Air Force Base, 5th Bomb Wing Public Affairs.)

Two

906th Air Refueling Squadron September 23, 1959–January 1994

The Strategic Air Command's 4136th Strategic Wing was assigned to Minot Air Force Base in September 1958 with the 906th Air Refueling Squadron; the 4136th Combat Defense Squadron followed on June 1, 1959. Minot Air Force Base personnel witnessed the arrival of the first KC-135A, named *Miss Minot*, on September 23, 1959. The squadron's KC-135As began the strategic jet era in North Dakota, as they were the first tactical or strategic jet aircraft permanently assigned in the state. With the arrival of the Stratotankers, maintenance and operations crews increased training and technical knowledge of the KC-135A. The first Stratotanker crew trained by the wing upgraded to Strategic Air Command combat-ready operational status on October 31, 1959. By December 31, 1959, the 4136th Strategic Wing had nine combat-ready tanker aircrews. With training completed for aerial refueling missions, the wing had to prepare for the arrival of the Boeing B-52H Stratofortress bomber. On July 1, 1975, an additional Strategic Air Command authorization for the 5th Bomb Wing increased the number of KC-135As from 15 to 18. The 906th Air Refueling Squadron supported the Permanent Tanker Task Force, the Pacific Tanker Task Force, and the European and Alaska Tanker Task Forces while also flying worldwide missions in 1978 in support of allied aircraft and Strategic Air Command bombers. The squadron supported US combat operations in Southeast Asia from 1968 to 1978 and Southwest Asia from 1990 to 1991. The squadron transferred to Grand Forks Air Force Base on January 39, 1994, after upgrading to the KC-135R.

A formerly classified event was the temporary assignment of a U-2 detachment of three aircraft to Minot Air Force Base in September 1958. Detachment 2, 4080th Strategic Reconnaissance Wing, from Laughlin Air Force Base, Texas, arrived as part of Operation Crew Flight to conduct high-altitude weather reconnaissance studies for traces of radioactive debris from tests of US special weapons projects. The detachment was scheduled for nine months but remained on Minot Air Force Base for 18 months.

This Boeing KC-135A Stratotanker is on display at the South Dakota Air and Space Museum, outside of Ellsworth Air Force Base. This variant was used at Minot Air Force Base to support B-52H bombers. (Author's collection.)

The first KC-135A assigned to the 906th Air Refueling Squadron landed at Minot Air Force Base on September 23, 1959. It was named *Miss Minot* and was christened in a ceremony on the flight line. (Courtesy Minot Air Force Base, 5th Bomb Wing Public Affairs.)

Two 906th Air Refueling Squadron KC-135As are cocked (ready for immediate launch) on Strategic Air Command 15-minute nuclear alert/launch on the alert pad (referred to as the "Christmas Tree") off the south end of the runway. The tanker and bomber alert crew facility (the "Moe Hole") is located to the right. The entire area was under 5th Bomb Wing Security Forces personnel, requiring verified authorized identification badges to enter the area. Vehicles parked in front of the alert facility are for the assigned aircrews. A 5th Bomb Wing B-52H is parked in the last parking area to the left with others on the opposite side. (Courtesy Minot Air Force Base, 5th Bomb Wing Public Affairs.)

This dramatic head-on photograph shows a KC-135A taking off using water injection to augment the thrust of the turbojet engines on a training alert using the minimum interval take-off (MITO) exercise, designed to launch the ground-alert nuclear deterrent force within 15 minutes. A B-52 is on the taxiway, ready to turn on to the runway for immediate takeoff. This exercise was conducted at Barksdale Air Force Base, Louisiana, following established Strategic Air Command alert procedures as used at Minot Air Force Base. (Courtesy Barksdale Air Force Base, Air Force Global Strike Command Historian.)

The KC-135A is a multirole aircraft; the upward-opening cargo door allows cargo to be loaded into the tanker and secured with straps, along with hauling squadron personnel to its deployed location. The 906th Air Refueling Squadron conducted a deployment away from Minot Air Force Base to Andersen Air Force Base, Guam, in 1982. (Courtesy Minot Air Force Base, 5th Bomb Wing Historian.)

The 906th Air Refueling Squadron deployed to Southeast Asia during the Vietnam War. The three aircraft in front of the tanker are McDonnell Douglas F-4 fighter/bombers; two Republic F-105D fighter/bombers are in the background. (Courtesy Department of Defense, Department of the Air Force Historian.)

This closeup view is of a KC-135A Stratotanker on display at the Kansas Air Museum at Wichita. The Stratotankers were removed from operational service as they reached maximum service life, with some transferred to air museums. (Author's collection.)

One of the most classified events at Minot Air Force Base was the arrival and operation of three Lockheed U-2 Dragon Lady top-secret photo-reconnaissance/electronic surveillance aircraft. (Courtesy Department of Defense, Department of the Air Force Historian.)

Detachment 2's mission was flying at high altitude to collect air samples to determine the composition of aboveground nuclear detonations by the Soviet Union and United States. Though the U-2 looks like a glider, two engine inlets provide air for one turbojet engine. (Courtesy Department of Defense, Department of Air Force Historian.)

While operating at Minot Air Force Base for 18 months, the U-2 was equipped with the air sampling sensors seen on the left side of the fuselage, below the engine inlet in front of the centerline landing gear. The three U-2s conducted high-altitude weather reconnaissance for traces of radioactive debris from aboveground nuclear tests. The special sampling equipment was a collector for the High-Altitude Sample Program (HASP). This was a highly classified program, and the relatively isolated Minot Air Force Base was ideal for concealing the three U-2s inside hangars during the day, launching them, and recovering them without announcement. The sounds of jet aircraft on the base raised no indications of this sensitive mission. It is an important story of the Cold War, as the United States conducted nuclear tests to develop deterrent weapons for the conflict against the Soviet Union. (Courtesy Department of Defense, Department of the Air Force Historian.)

Three

5TH FIGHTER-INTERCEPTOR SQUADRON

FEBRUARY 1, 1960–JULY 1, 1985

The detonation of the Soviet Union's first atomic bomb in 1949 gave concern to the US political and military leadership, who believed the nation was under imminent threat of nuclear attack. Air Defense Command began building fighter-interceptor bases along the US-Canadian border. The 433rd Fighter-Interceptor Squadron was assigned to the newly constructed Minot Air Force Base, equipped with Convair F-106A Delta Darts operating from the base from February 1960 to April 1985.

The Cuban Missile Crisis (October 14–28, 1962), which threatened nuclear war between the United States and the Soviet Union, impacted the 433rd Fighter-Interceptor Squadron. The base maintained four F-106As on Air Defense Command alert on the south end of the runway inside a double complex of two-bay alert hangars. Pres. John F. Kennedy sent a repositioning order to the squadron, moving the four F-106As to Fargo International Airport. A little-known part of this repositioning was that each carried an AIR-2A Genie rocket armed with a 1.5-kiloton warhead. Once at Fargo, the four F-106As were ready to be launched to intercept any incoming Soviet bombers attempting to pass over Canada to attack the United States.

The squadron reached a strength of 24 F-106As, two F-106Bs (twin-seat transition trainers), and three T-33As (for pilot proficiency and liaison). In 1968, the squadron flew electronic measure intercepts against twin-engine B-57 medium bombers and eight-engine B-52 heavy bombers, which flew predicted penetration routes of Russian bombers to provide realistic Cold War air intercept training.

In 1975, the squadron deployed to Hahn Air Base, Federal Republic of Germany, to participate in the Air Defense Command's first fighter deployment to Exercise Gold Fire 75 to demonstrate the command's ability to rapidly move fighter aircraft to counter a possible Soviet air threat.

On December 4, 1984, the squadron began replacing its F-106s with the advanced McDonnell Douglas F-15 Eagle. The squadron only operated the F-15 until mid-1985, when the squadron was inactivated and its aircraft transferred to the 101st Fighter-Interceptor Squadron at Otis Air Force Base, Massachusetts.

Pictured is a Convair F-106A, an all-weather supersonic interceptor designed to attack an unknown hostile airborne threat attempting to penetrate US airspace. The aircraft is on display at the Montana Air National Guard 120th Airlift Wing at Great Falls International Airport. (Author's collection.)

Shown is an AIR-2A Genie rocket, which could be armed with a 1.5-kiloton warhead, on its missile transporter and erector loader for positioning the missile inside the center-mounted internal weapons bay of an F-106A. The missile is on display at South Dakota Air and Space Museum, adjacent to Ellsworth Air Force Base. (Author's collection.)

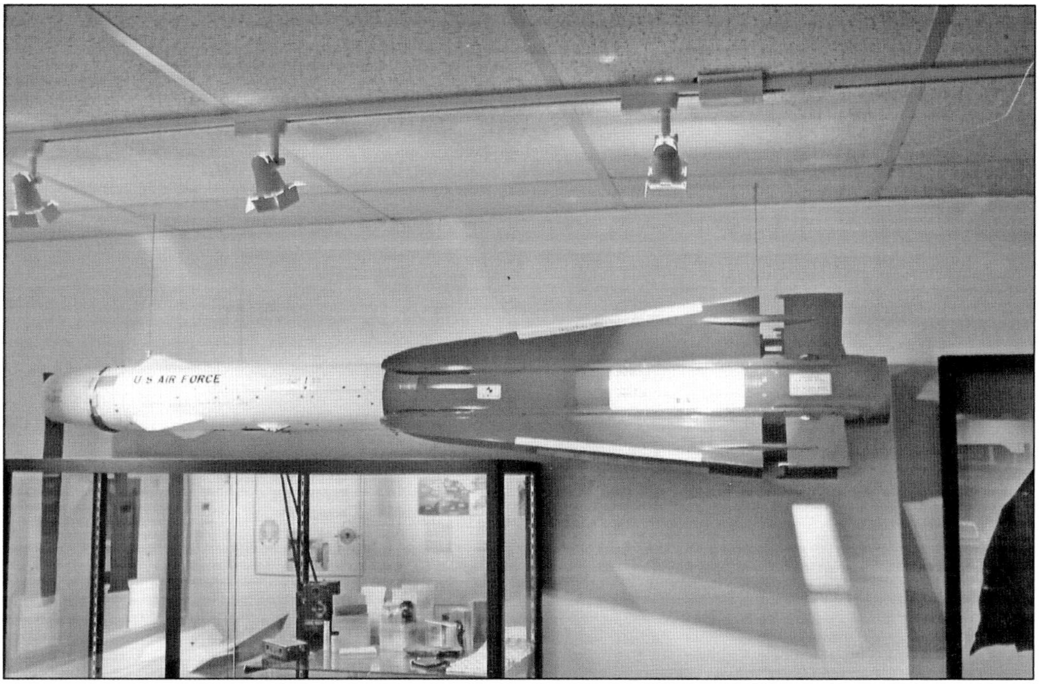

The F-106A carried four conventional-warhead Falcon air intercept missiles, two with radar guidance and two with heat-seeking guidance. This AIM-4F/4G Falcon is on display at the South Dakota Air and Space Museum, adjacent to Ellsworth Air Force Base. (Author's collection.)

A 5th Fighter-Interceptor Squadron F-106A is pictured on the Minot Air Force Base flight line with its canopy closed. The absence of ground support equipment indicates that this aircraft is not scheduled for a training flight. (Courtesy Minot Air Force Base, 5th Bomb Wing Historian.)

An F-106A of the 5th Fighter-Interceptor Squadron is on the flight line during the winter. The canopy is open with the pilot access ladder in place. There is no ground support equipment positioned around the aircraft at this time. (Courtesy Minot Air Force Base, 5th Bomb Wing Historian.)

The 5th Fighter-Interceptor Squadron, Air Defense Command, created a spectacular front cover for Minot Air Force Base's *Minot Guide*, which contained base history, general information on units assigned, and office phone numbers. (Courtesy Minot Air Force Base, 5th Bomb Wing Historian.)

Due to Air Defense Command alert requirements, there were often not enough aircraft for squadron pilots to acquire monthly flying hours, so they flew Lockheed T-33As. This aircraft is on display at the Montana Air National Guard 120th Airlift Wing at Great Falls International Airport. (Author's collection.)

A Convair F-106A Delta Dart is on the concrete aircraft parking ramp outside the Convair Aircraft production plant at Palmdale, California. From left to right are one Genie rocket and a combination of AIM-4G and AIM-4F radar-guided and heat-seeking missiles. (Courtesy Minot Air Force Base, 5th Bomb Wing Historian.)

For pilot training and cockpit proficiency, the 5th Fighter-Interceptor Squadron had cockpit trainers. This F-106A cockpit trainer is on display at the South Dakota Air and Space Museum adjacent to Ellsworth Air Force Base. (Author's collection.)

A 5th Fighter-Interceptor Squadron F-106A is on the Minot Air Force Base flight line with maintenance personnel preparing the aircraft for a training flight. (Courtesy Minot Air Force Base, 5th Bomb Wing Historian.)

Two 5th Fighter-Interceptor Squadron F-106s are airborne after launching from Minot Air Force Base on a training mission. The aircraft were photographed from a third squadron F-106A. (Courtesy Minot Air Force Base, 5th Bomb Wing Historian.)

Aviation artist Stan Stokes provided a copy of his *Cold War Encounter*, picturing what an air intercept by an F-106A of a penetrating Soviet Tu-95 Bear bomber might look like somewhere in the mountains. (Courtesy Stan Stokes.)

An F-106A intercepts a Soviet Tu-95 bomber in international airspace off the coast of Alaska. (Courtesy Department of Defense, Department of the Air Force Historian.)

A former 5th Fighter-Interceptor Squadron F-106A is pictured in the desert open storage area at the Air Force Aerospace Maintenance and Regeneration Center, Davis-Monthan Air Force Base, Arizona. The aircraft has gone through a complete cocoon process. (Author's collection.)

This former 5th Fighter-Interceptor Squadron F-106A, with all internal equipment removed, is on display at Minot Air Force Base. (Author's collection.)

For a short time, the 5th Fighter-Interceptor Squadron was equipped with the McDonnell Douglas F-15A Eagle. It is a twin-engine, high-performance, all-weather, air-superiority fighter. (Courtesy Minot Air Force Base, 5th Bomb Wing Historian.)

This McDonnell Douglas F-15A Eagle, seen close up from in front, is on display at the Montana Air National Guard 120th Airlift Wing at Great Falls International Airport. (Author's collection.)

When the 5th Fighter-Interceptor Squadron was inactivated at Minot Air Force Base in 1985, its F-15As were transferred to the 101st Fighter-Interceptor Squadron at Otis Air Force Base, Massachusetts. (Courtesy 101st Fighter-Interceptor Squadron Public Affairs.)

Four

786TH AIRCRAFT AND WARNING SQUADRON 1978–1997

Minot Air Force Station was built 16 miles south of Minot Air Force Base to the west of US Highway 83. The radar station operated until 1978, transitioning to a communications station to support Minot Air Force Base until 1997. It is one of the few radar stations remaining partially intact. It was built and operated as the first Air Force radar station in North Dakota, before initial operations of either Minot or Grand Forks Air Force Base. It was in the final group of 23 radar stations built by Air Defense Command, activated on May 20, 1951, and began search operations in April 1952. It initially operated as a ground intercept and warning station. Its primary assigned mission was to direct fighter-interceptors to within visual contact with an unidentified aircraft. The squadron's radars were frequently upgraded as more modern and capable electronics became available.

To augment the Air Defense Command mission, the North American Air Defense Command developed and deployed the semi-automated ground environment (SAGE) system, one of which was based at Minot Air Force Base. Construction of the huge, windowless, blast-resistant concrete building began in July 1958. The building held two first-generation IBM 275-ton computers, each with 50,000 vacuum tubes, installed in 1960. The building was designed to survive a nearby nuclear detonation. The Department of Defense officially revealed the existence of this new system on January 17, 1956. Minot Air Force Station was the center for a large network of Gap Filler radars, forwarding collected information to Minot Air Force Base using telephones to report possible hostile threats.

The threat from Russian intercontinental ballistic missiles to Minot Air Force Base and other bases led to reductions of the concrete blockhouse computer buildings. The Minot facility was deactivated on May 15, 1963. The 786th Radar Squadron met its operational end on June 30, 1976.

This aerial photograph of Minot Air Force Station shows the two dome radar towers, barracks, the power and heat plant, support buildings, and housing units. US Highway 83 is in the background. (Courtesy Minot Air Force Base, 5th Bomb Wing Historian.)

A closeup view shows the installation's primary search radar. The height-finder radar is in the background. The radar unit was protected from weather by the dome on top of the concrete tower. (Courtesy Minot Air Force Base, 5th Bomb Wing.)

The four-story SAGE building at Minot Air Force Base was enormous and hardened to withstand a nuclear detonation overpressure of five pounds per square inch. (Courtesy Minot Air Force Base, 5th Bomb Wing Public Affairs.)

In 1952, the security entrance into Minot Air Force Station was controlled by a single, wood-frame guard shack and vehicles entered from US Highway 83. (Courtesy Minot Air Force Base, 5th Bomb Wing Historian.)

Pictured is the location where a Cold War guard shack, now removed, once stood. The perimeter security fence remains. (Author's collection.)

The radar station's dining hall is to the right, with the orderly room to the left. The radar station's flagpole is to one side and in front of the orderly room. (Courtesy Minot Air Force Base, 5th Bomb Wing Historian.)

Pictured is the station's steam heating plant. The radar station's buildings were connected by underground pipes to provide heat during North Dakota's cold winters. (Author's collection.)

One of the six two-story concrete-block enlisted barracks on the Air Force station, this was built to the standard 1950s US Army Corps of Engineers plans used initially by the Air Force in Cold War construction. (Author's collection.)

Electronic equipment from around 1959 is pictured inside the base of the search radar tower. The ceiling was full of air intakes and exhausts to cool the vacuum-tube computers inside. (Courtesy Minot Air Force Base, 5th Bomb Wing Historian.)

The modernized 1970s communications center was equipped with a roof-mounted central air-conditioning unit to support the communications facility. (Author's collection.)

This section of the former accompanied housing unit was sold to local residents. (Author's collection.)

The motor pool area is seen around the 1970s with a garage to the left and assorted vehicles parked nearby. In the background is a concrete two-story enlisted barracks. (Courtesy Minot Air Force Base, 5th Bomb Wing Historian.)

In 2014, remains of the radar station's search radar building show the concrete ground structure, the framework radar tower rising up from the building's center, and the auxiliary power station in the background in case of loss of commercial power. (Author's collection.)

Shown is a concrete two-story unaccompanied enlisted barracks required to maintain 24-hour radar search operations. The building is now used for general storage. (Author's collection.)

Remaining onsite military housing at the radar complex is one story and typical of 1950s construction. (Author's collection.)

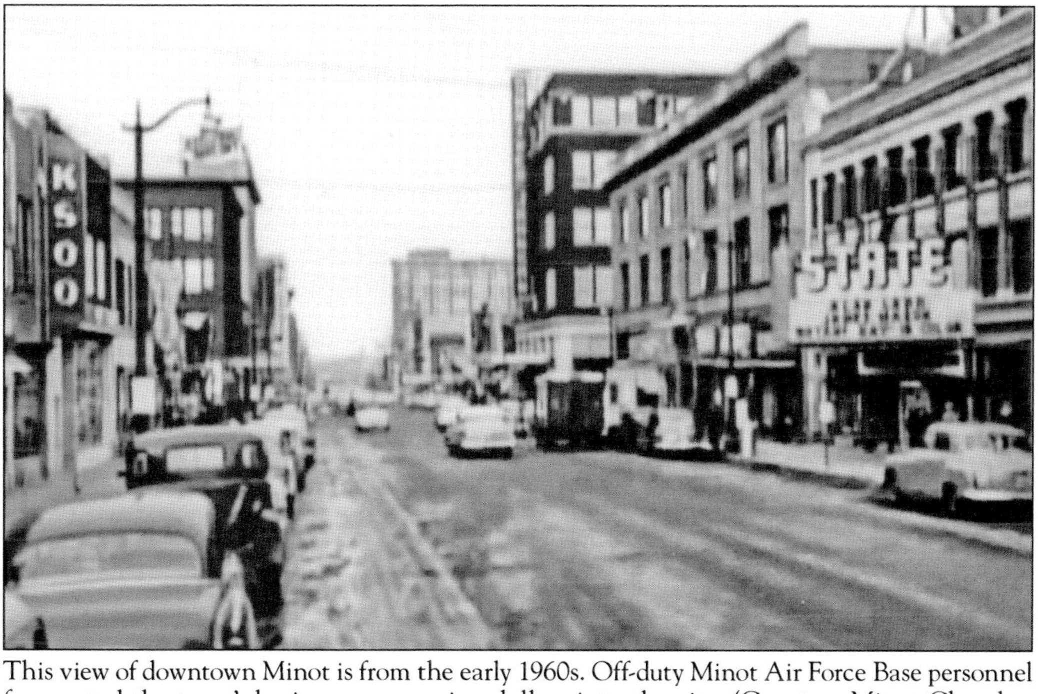

This view of downtown Minot is from the early 1960s. Off-duty Minot Air Force Base personnel frequented the town's businesses, pumping dollars into the city. (Courtesy Minot Chamber of Commerce.)

These are the remaining concrete pillars that supported diesel fuel tanks for the auxiliary power plant. The on-site plant provided uninterrupted electricity for the site's radar. (Author's collection.)

This view was taken from the south end of the Air Force station looking north. In the foreground are the housing complex and two radar domes. US Highway 83 is to the right, leading to Minot, 16 miles to the north. (Courtesy Minot Air Force Base, 5th Bomb Wing Historian.)

Five

5TH BOMB WING 1961–PRESENT

The first B-52H to land at Minot Air Force Base in 1961 was named *Peace Persuader*. On July 25, 1968, the 5th Bomb Wing was activated. Even though Minot Air Force Base was a Strategic Air Command nuclear base, its aircrews, not the B-52Hs, were often deployed to fight in the air war in Southeast Asia, flying B-52Ds after training at Castle Air Force Base, California.

On August 29–30, 2007, personnel of the 5th Bomb Wing made a nuclear weapons security mistake by loading six live but nonoperational W-80-1 nuclear warheads onto six of 12 cruise missiles to be flown to Barksdale Air Force, Louisiana, for deactivation. As a result, nuclear security procedures were tightened.

On August 21, 2011, a 5th Bomb Wing B-52H with a four-officer aircrew completed a historic flight from Minot Air Force Base over the geographic North Pole, landing at the Moscow International Air and Space Aviation Salon. Russian Air Force officers were impressed by how well maintained the B-52H was.

In May 2012, the 5th Bomb Wing flew a B-52H on a global power demonstration flight to Germany and back to Minot Air Force Base. The Stratofortress was refueled four times, once from a French air force tanker.

Minot Air Force Base reached another historic event on July 12, 2015, celebrating the 60th anniversary of the base's ground-breaking ceremony. The runway constructed in 1975 lived beyond its 30-year life expectancy, requiring the center section to be dug up and replaced in 2014. The wing's B-52Hs deployed to the 28th Bomb Wing at Ellsworth Air Force Base, South Dakota, during repair work.

In December 2015, the wing's B-52Hs flew for the first time on the expanded Powder River Training Complex in Wyoming, allowing Air Force Global Strike Command's bombers to exercise combat scenarios against simulated worldwide target areas.

On May 19, 2016, a 5th Bomb Wing B-52H was destroyed in a fiery crash on Andersen Air Force Base, Guam, with the seven crewmembers surviving.

A 5th Bomb Wing B-52H takes off from Minot Air Force Base. The flight line and hangars are to the right. The photograph was taken from the runway control tower. (Courtesy Minot Air Force Base, 5th Bomb Wing Public Affairs.)

A B-52H is pictured in August 2014 parked in the former alert pad area with covers over the intakes to protect the engines from weather and blowing debris. The alert area's double security fence is visible, along with security warning signs. (Author's collection.)

The Cold War–era alert building, referred to as the Moe Hole, is to the right side of the aircraft taxiway into and out of the alert parking area. Alert crews accessed the base in assigned vehicles to respond to the klaxon for scramble to their aircraft. (Author's collection.)

The aircraft alert area was heavily guarded by armed Security Forces personnel. A steel guard tower, with a glass observation platform on top, provides an unobstructed 360-degree view of the alert area below along with high-intensity light poles. (Author's collection.)

Another 5th Bomb Wing B-52H is parked inside the former alert security area. (Author's collection.)

This photograph shows the wide variety of weapons the B-52H can carry, from nuclear to conventional. (Courtesy Minot Air Force Base, 5th Bomb Wing Public Affairs.)

Pictured are 5th Bomb Wing B-52Hs taxiing to the end of the runway on Minot Air Force Base to practice an alert MITO. This is required to maintain proficiency if the wing resumes nuclear alert. (Courtesy Minot Air Force Base, 5th Bomb Wing Public Affairs.)

From 1961 until 1976, the B-52H was armed with the Hound Dog, a stand-off air-to-surface attack missile. It was designed to increase the bomber's capability to attack heavily defended Soviet targets. (Courtesy Minot Air Force Base, 5th Bomb Wing Public Affairs.)

This closeup photograph shows a restored Hound Dog missile on its munitions transporter. The yellow-painted steel cradle can raise or lower the Hound Dog missile onto or down from the B-52H's underwing pylon. (Author's collection.)

On September 27, 1991, Pres. George H.W. Bush ordered an end to 24-hour, 15-minute bomber ground alert operations, including for the B-52Hs on Minot Air Force Base. A munitions transporter, designed to hold six missiles, is positioned underneath the left wing of a B-52H, downloading the missiles to comply with President Bush's orders. (Courtesy Minot Air Force Base, 5th Bomb Wing Public affairs.)

This closeup view of the right-wing pylon shows six air-launched cruise missiles and a fully extended munitions transporter beginning the download process. The missiles were towed to the weapons storage area for secure storage. (Courtesy Minot Air Force Base, 5th Bomb Wing Public Affairs.)

During the winter, snow and extreme cold are a problem. Two maintenance personnel are pushing a work platform through the snow in front of an aircraft, with an access door open for work inside the aircraft. (Courtesy Minot Air Force Base, 5th Bomb Wing Public Affairs.)

A snow-covered B-52H is on the parking ramp prior to a training flight during the winter. Its control surfaces must be deiced for proper flight operations and repeatedly checked prior to takeoff for additional deicing. (Courtesy Minot Air Force Base, 5th Bomb Wing Public Affairs.)

Even during a snowstorm, with heavy blowing snow across the aircraft parking ramp, maintenance work cannot stop. A tractor tow vehicle is positioned in front of a B-52H with a tow connector to move the aircraft. (Courtesy Minot Air Force Base, 5th Bomb Wing Public Affairs.)

Extremes of winter weather, shown in this photograph, can hit Minot Air Force Base. These B-52Hs are covered with snow, with high winds creating a near whiteout on the flight line, referred to as "zero-zero visibility." (Courtesy Minot Air Force Base, 5th Bomb Wing Public Affairs.)

Even after the September 1991 end of 24-hour nuclear alert, the 5th Bomb Wing must conduct periodic training for nuclear operations, including MITO. This is designed to launch B-52Hs in the shortest time, clearing the base to a safe area for refueling. (Courtesy Minot Air Force Base, 5th Bomb Wing Public Affairs.)

In this tail view of B-52Hs on the parallel taxiway, each maintains a precise distance from the aircraft in front prior to turning onto the runway and immediate takeoff. (Courtesy Minot Air Force Base, 5th Bomb Wing Public Affairs.)

One B-52H is on the runway with pilots adding takeoff power to the eight engines. The wings come off the runway first, with the landing gear coming off next as the bomber reaches takeoff speed. (Courtesy Minot Air Force Base, 5th Bomb Wing Public Affairs.)

A B-52H is seen after takeoff, providing a view of the landing gear with flaps down, exhaust from the eight engines trailing the aircraft. (Courtesy Minot Air Force Base, 5th Bomb Wing Public Affairs.)

This bottom view of a B-52H gaining altitude after takeoff shows the flaps extended from the underside of the wing for lift. (Courtesy Minot Air Force Base, 5th Bomb Wing Public Affairs.)

As B-52Hs clear Minot Air Force Base, engine exhaust provides a dramatic photograph of the Stratofortresses' MITO exercise. (Courtesy Minot Air Force Base, 5th Bomb Wing Public Affairs.)

To perform maintenance on the 5th Bomb Wing's B-52Hs, large aircraft hangars were built. A B-52H was towed nose-first into the hangar, with all except the tail inside. The hangar doors were closed, sealing the aircraft in. (Author's collection.)

Shown is the back side of a B-52H hangar, with garage-type doors allowing maintenance vehicles and movement of aircraft repair parts into and out of the hangar. Parking space for vehicles is provided off the aircraft parking ramp. (Author's collection.)

With the tail section of a B-52H sticking out, hangar doors are closed around the aircraft's fuselage. (Author's collection.)

Pictured is the vehicle access road between a row of B-52H hangars. This allows access to the B-52Hs inside the hangars without movement on the controlled flight line operations areas. (Author's collection.)

The Cold War hangars could not hold the entire B-52H out of extreme winter weather. On March 18, 2015, the 80,000-square-foot B-52H Phase Dock (hangar) was operational, holding two B-52Hs. (Courtesy Minot Air Force Base, 5th Bomb Wing Public Affairs.)

The new runway control tower's height provides a close view of a B-52H conducting a flyby of the tower to check on the aircraft's landing gear and flap position. Two B-52Hs are on the flight line, with a hangar to the left. (Courtesy Minot Air Force Base, 5th Bomb Wing Public Affairs.)

The view from the control tower of the Minot Air Force Base runway is exceptional due to its height, which provides a closeup view of this B-52H flying by. (Courtesy Minot Air Force Base, 5th Bomb Wing Public Affairs.)

After a training mission, a B-52H lands on Minot Air Force Base's runway, with a yellow drogue parachute deployed from the rear to slow down the aircraft. (Courtesy Minot Air Force Base, 5th Bomb Wing Public Affairs.)

This closeup, left side, head-on view of a B-52H shows its drogue parachute deployed and wing flaps fully extended to slow the aircraft after landing. (Courtesy Minot Air Force Base, 5th Bomb Wing Public Affairs.)

A ground crewman with his arms crossed indicates to the B-52H's pilots to shut off the bomber's engines after taxiing to the parking pad at the conclusion of a training mission. (Courtesy Minot Air Force Base, 5th Bomb Wing Public Affairs.)

Pictured is a row of parked B-52Hs on the north end of the parking ramp on Minot Air Force Base. The aircraft are positioned for access by maintenance personnel, aircrew prior to takeoff on training flights, and flight line security. (Author's collection.)

This closeup view shows B-52Hs on the parking ramp. In the left background is the aircraft ramp Security Forces guard tower. The guard tower's height provides Security Forces personnel an unobstructed view of the B-52Hs below. (Courtesy Minot Air Force Base, 5th Bomb Wing Public Affairs.)

Reconstruction of Minot Air Force Base's center runway section, replacing the 1957 runway, was one of the Air Force's top infrastructure projects, according to a 2011 Air Force Civil Engineering Support Agency study. (Courtesy Minot Air Force Base, 5th Bomb Wing Public Affairs.)

It took a large amount of equipment and manpower to pave Minot Air Force Base's center runway section. (Courtesy Minot Air Force Base, 5th Bomb Wing Public Affairs.)

Contractors and inspectors walk over the completed runway center section looking for visible irregularities in the surface composition, texture, and conformity to contract specifications. (Courtesy Minot Air Force Base, 5th Bomb Wing Public Affairs.)

B-52H pilots try to perform a touchdown of all four landing gear trucks onto the runway at the same time, leveling off prior to touchdown, but it does not always work out. This B-52H is nearing touchdown position. (Courtesy Minot Air Force Base, 5th Bomb Wing Public Affairs.)

A B-52H passes underneath two base fire trucks' fire suppression nozzles spraying water streams into the air over the aircraft parking ramp entrance, forming a visible water arch. (Courtesy Minot Air Force Base, 5th Bomb Wing Public Affairs.)

Personnel assigned to the 5th Bomb Wing on Minot Air Force Base assisted the city of Minot emergency agencies during the disastrous flood on June 23, 2011, when the Souris River overtopped the levees, forcing the evacuation of 11,000 residents. (Courtesy Minot Air Force Base, 5th Bomb Wing Public Affairs.)

Low-lying areas of Minot flooded; 5th Bomb Wing Public Affairs assisted in stacking sandbags for flood protection. (Courtesy Minot Air Force Base, 5th Bomb Wing Public Affairs.)

Minot Air Force Base B-52Hs, while flying training missions, frequently conduct flyovers after the national anthem is played at public events like this Minnesota Twins baseball game. (Courtesy Minot Air Force Base, 5th Bomb Wing Public Affairs.)

On May 19, 2016, a Minot Air Force Base 5th Bomb Wing B-52H crashed on Andersen Air Force Base while landing when a flock of birds was sucked into the engines, destroying the aircraft. (Courtesy Andersen Air Force Base, 9th Operations Group Public Affairs.)

This Minot Air Force Base 5th Bomb Wing Public Affairs photograph shows a B-52H taking off from the runway at sunset. (Courtesy Minot Air Force Base, 5th Bomb Wing Public Affairs.)

This B-52H, after taking off from Minot Air Force Base, is heading into the sunset, providing a remarkable photograph. (Courtesy Minot Air Force Base, 5th Bomb Wing Public Affairs.)

Minot Air Force Base held its first airshow in seven years on August 13, 2016. A 5th Bomb Wing B-52H on the flight line allowed visitors to closely inspect the Stratofortress and wait in line to climb into the bomber's cockpit. (Courtesy Minot Air Force Base, 5th Bomb Wing Public Affairs.)

This photograph, taken from the runway control tower looking toward the Minot Air Force Base flight line, shows a B-52H to the left and a KC-135R to the right. In the background, between the B-52H and KC-135R, is the Thunderbirds' No. 7 Falcon jet on display prior to the six-jet Thunderbirds Aerial Demonstration Team performing for the gathered crowd. (Courtesy Minot Air Force Base, 5th Bomb Wing Pubic Affairs.)

On October 27, 2015, the Department of Defense announced that the Northrop Grumman Corporation would build the Long Range Strike Bomber, designated the B-21. (Courtesy Department of Defense, Department of the Air Force Long Range Strike Bomber Office.)

Minot Air Force base is well-suited to replace its 1960s-produced Boeing B-52H Stratofortress with the B-21. (Courtesy Department of Defense, Department of the Air Force Long Range Strike Bomber Office.)

Six

Weapons Storage Area 1961–Present

Initial construction of munitions magazines for the Minot Air Force Base Weapons Storage Area followed plans provided by the US Army Corps of Engineers. These were earth-covered storage igloos. In the event of an accidental explosion, the resulting blast would be directed upward, through the six-inch-thick concrete roof; the concrete walls' thickness increased to 18 inches at ground level, protecting adjacent storage igloos. Later construction in the weapons storage area used Air Force plans for specialized weapons storage.

The storage area has a single entry gate. The entire area is secured by a double eight-foot-high chain-link fence topped with concertina barbed wire. A perimeter road is patrolled by Security Forces personnel. The security area is lit by high-intensity floodlights, with their poles and other measures providing anti-helicopter intrusion barriers. A steel tower with an enclosed viewing room on top provides the Security Forces an unobstructed view of the storage area's 33 structures.

A map of Minot Air Force Base is blank where the weapons storage area is located. The area is shielded from ground view by trees and shrubs along US Highway 83 at the base's perimeter. More shrubbery is along Bomber Boulevard and Missile Avenue. Even the hospital perimeter is similarly covered. Roving Security Forces personnel patrol the exterior of the storage area to maintain visual security.

The storage area secures nuclear weapons that can be loaded into the B-52Hs and warheads for the Minuteman III intercontinental ballistic missile. To man the storage area, the Air Force has a dedicated career field of professionals to ship, receive, build, test, operate, secure, inspect, store, and perform required weapons maintenance.

The weapons storage area supports the Air Force Nuclear Security Program with specific processes, procedures, and responsibilities for obtaining and maintaining the certification of nuclear weapons systems, support equipment hardware and software, and classified facilities.

The following photographs look into the operations of the Minot Air Force Base Weapons Storage Area, which contributes to the security of the United States against possible external threats.

The Minot Air Force Base Weapons Storage Area is to the east of the former Cold War Christmas Tree nuclear bomber and tanker alert area, separated from base facilities for security considerations. (Courtesy US Geological Survey photographic archives.)

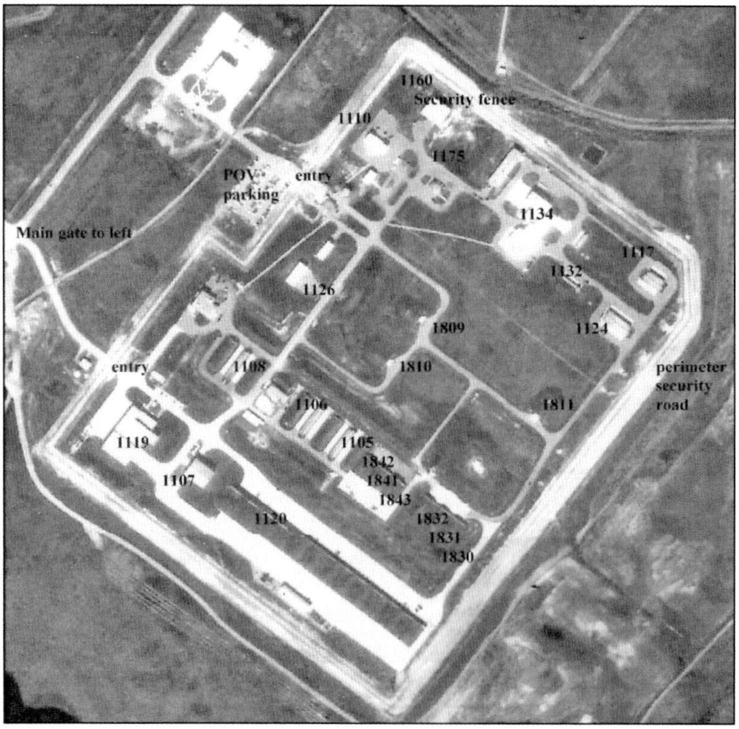

To assist in identifying the locations of buildings within the weapons storage area, building numbers have been added to this photograph from unclassified information at GlobalSecurity.org. (Courtesy US Geological Survey photographic archives.)

Paved or gravel surface patrol roads are located between and outside the high-security weapons storage. This conventional weapons storage area on Ellsworth Air Force Base shows double security fencing to prevent unauthorized intrusion. (Author's collection.)

The standard arched-roofed, reinforced, earth-covered storage magazine's entrance consists of double-leaf steel doors. Inside, two ventilators are in the head wall (door side), with a single ventilator in the rear wall to provide air exhaust exchange. (Author's collection.)

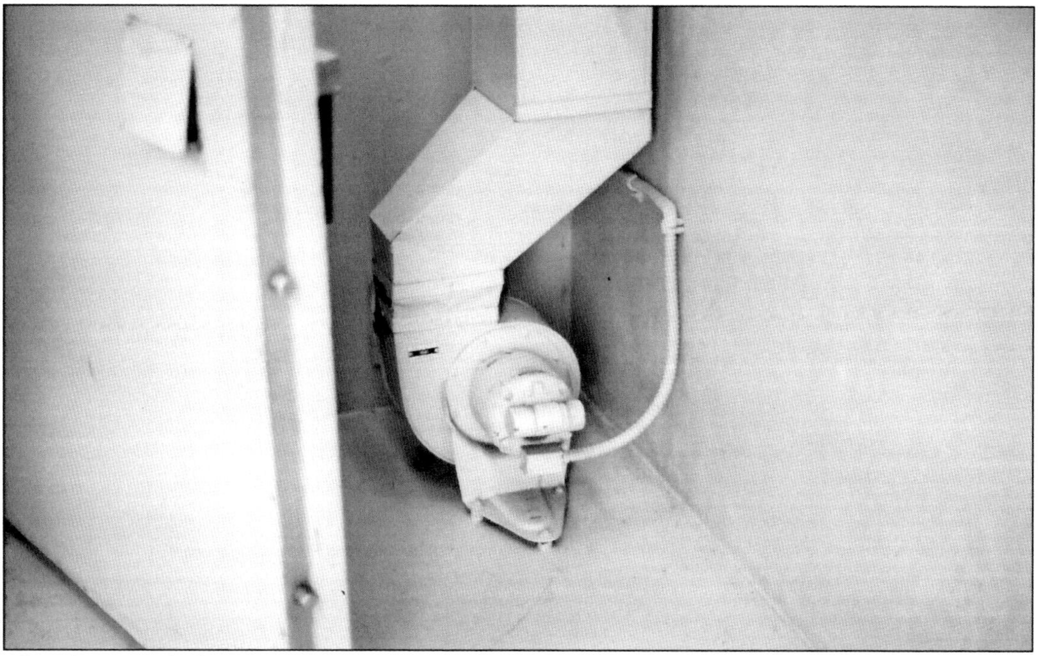

This photograph shows a 1960s-era ventilator inside the rear of a storage igloo using a one-third-horsepower motor to move air inside the earth-covered bunker. (Author's collection.)

Inside the weapons storage area is a steel tower topped with a glass-enclosed guard observation post with three windows on each side providing a clear view of the 33 buildings below. This type of security tower is standard at Air Force installations. (Author's collection.)

Weapons Storage Area Building 1107 (1) is used as a missile assembly and Minuteman missile checkout building. Building 119 (2) was constructed with a reinforced skeleton and concrete masonry walls for inspecting electrical and mechanical aprons for the Minuteman missile re-entry systems. (Courtesy US Geological Survey photographic archives.)

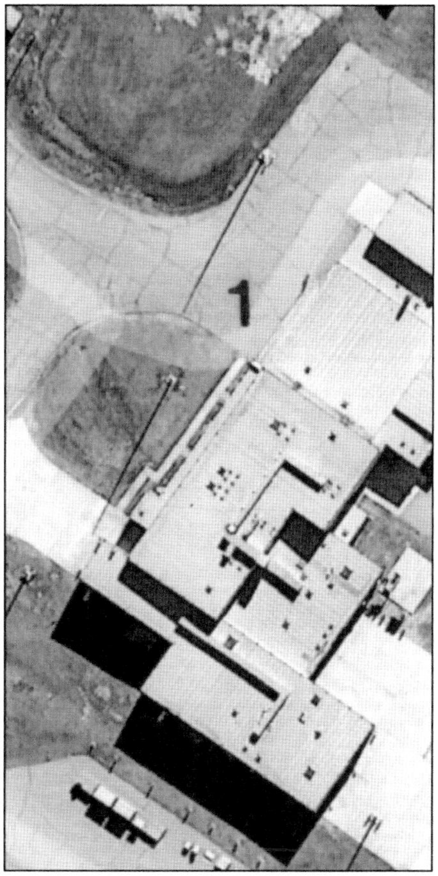

Building 1134 (1) is a large, multipurpose structure to conduct all aspects of missile storage, assembly testing, and refurbishment. A heavy crane can lift a rotary launcher with eight air-launched cruise missiles. (Courtesy US Geological Survey photographic archives.)

This overhead heavy-lift crane (used in the former nuclear weapons storage area on Ellsworth Air Force Base) is a standard design, as used in the Whiteman Air Force Base Weapons Storage Area, for loading and unloading operations, assembly, and maintenance functions. (Author's collection.)

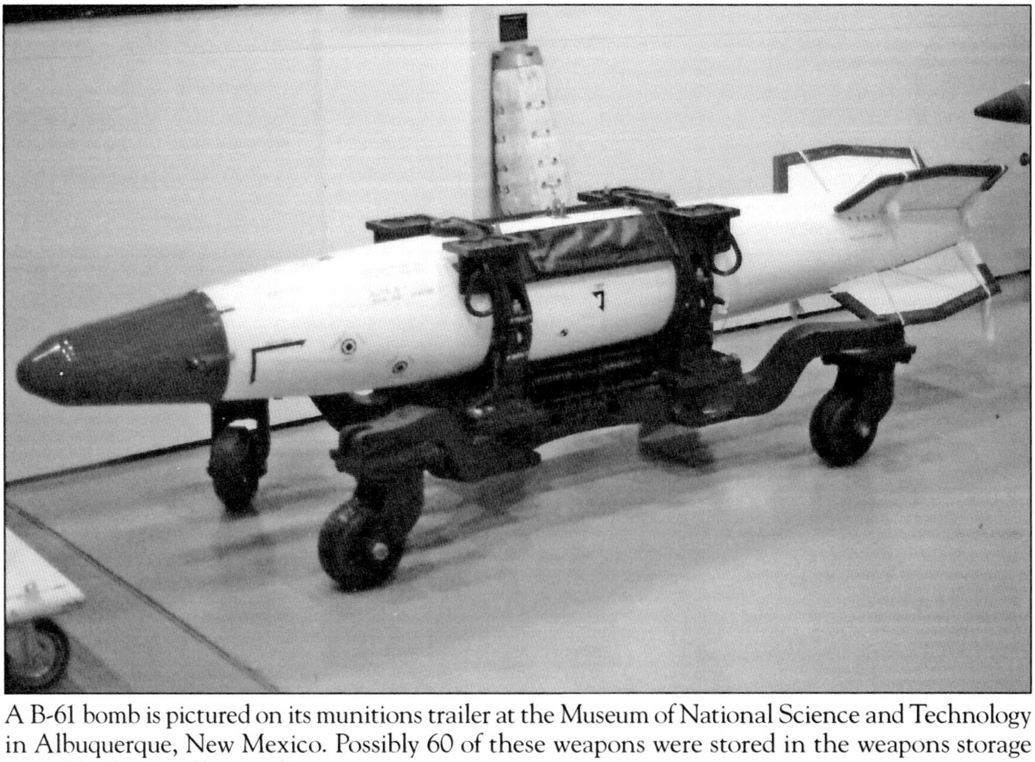

A B-61 bomb is pictured on its munitions trailer at the Museum of National Science and Technology in Albuquerque, New Mexico. Possibly 60 of these weapons were stored in the weapons storage area. (Author's collection.)

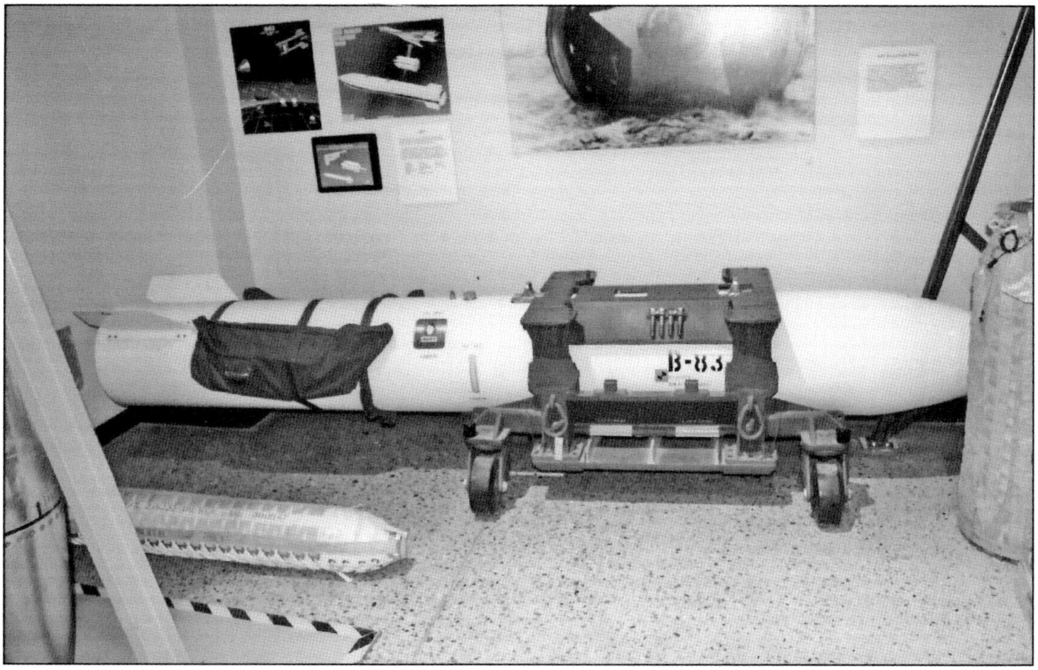

The Minot Air Force Base Weapons Storage Area possibly contains 90 B-83 gravity nuclear bombs, no longer loaded into the B-52H. This weapon is on its munitions transporter on display at the Museum of National Science and Technology in Albuquerque. (Author's collection.)

The weapons storage area possibly contains 100 W-80-1 air-launched cruise missile warheads. These weapons are being downloaded after bomber nuclear operations ended on Minot Air Force Base. (Courtesy Minot Air Force Base, 5th Bomb Wing Public Affairs.)

Initially, the wing's Minuteman IIIs required 450 W-78 warheads. Currently, each alert Minuteman III is armed with a single W-78 warhead inside the MK-11 reentry vehicle. This one is on display at the Whiteman Air Force Museum. (Author's collection.)

Early Cold War nuclear warheads used radioactive tritium gas triggers. Tritium triggers were stored in a standard, earth-covered munitions bunker with a distinctive modification—a tall air exhaust—in the 1960s. (Author's collection.)

Inside a tritium storage igloo, cubical steel storage shelves hold the canisters. These canisters are no longer used. Today, on Ellsworth Air Force Base, the storage igloos are used for general, non-nuclear material storage. (Author's collection.)

Building 1120 was originally constructed with six bays, each five feet, eight inches wide and eight feet, eight inches deep with a heavy steel door. It was enlarged to support Minuteman missile re-entry systems, like this building on Ellsworth Air Force Base. (Author's collection.)

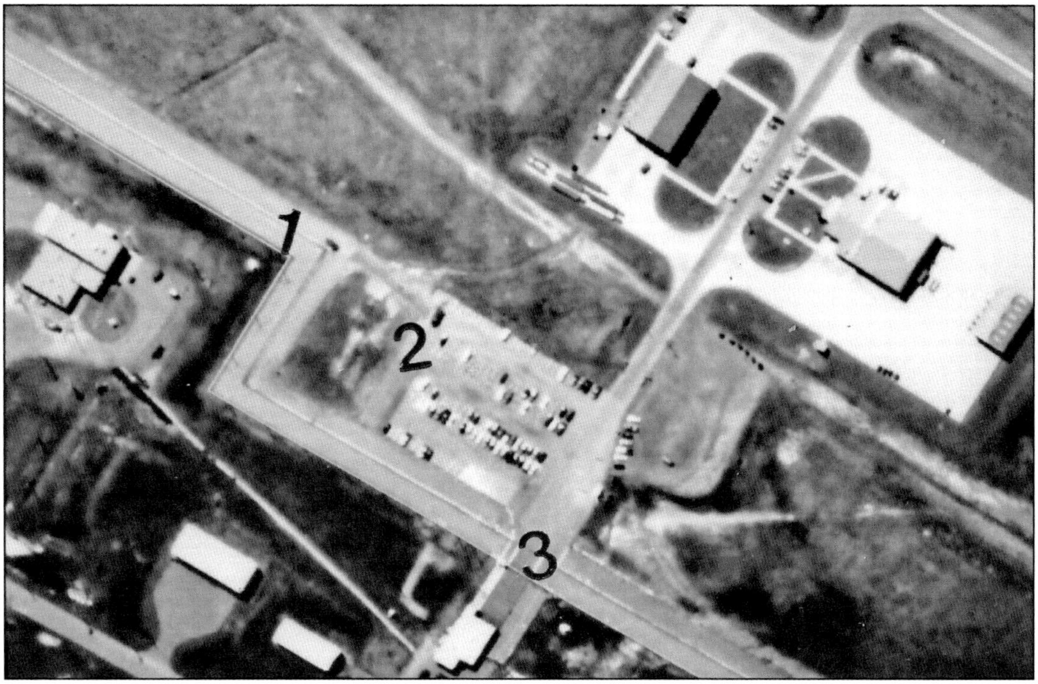

Double security fencing surrounds the Minot Air Force Base Weapons Storage Area. Civilian commercial vehicles (2) are parked in an exterior designated parking area. There is a single entry point (3) into the storage area. (Courtesy US Geological Survey photographic archives.)

This ground view shows the entrance to the former nuclear weapons storage area at Grand Forks Air Force Base, North Dakota. In August 2014, the storage area was in the midst of being demolished. The access gates are open, and the security building is to the right. (Author's collection.)

Seven

54TH HELICOPTER SQUADRON

MAY 1, 1993–PRESENT

The 54th Helicopter Squadron is a vital unit providing aerial support to Minot Air Force Base's 91st Missile Wing's Minuteman intercontinental ballistic missile launch facilities (silos) and missile alert facilities. The squadron supports Security Forces personnel to quickly and effectively respond to emergency conditions in the missile field. Its helicopters can transport Security Forces guarding missile convoys moving equipment, especially Minuteman nuclear warheads. The squadron's secondary missions include search and rescue of civilians in the surrounding area and transportation of distinguished visitors to locations within the large missile field. The squadron is nicknamed the "Rough Riders" and operates seven UH-1N Iroquois helicopters, nicknamed the "Huey."

The current threat is that a terrorist organization may attempt to attack a convoy from the nation's three missile wings. The September 11, 2001, terrorist attack forced an increase in security. The squadron's helicopters provide an eye in the sky for missile convoy protection. The wing's missile launch facilities are unmanned, with remote security monitoring to identify unauthorized entry. The Minuteman missiles in their underground launch tubes are virtually impregnable. The squadron's helicopters can rapidly deliver a tactical response team to counter any threats.

The squadron's mission is to ensure absolute integrity of the 91st Missile Wing's intercontinental ballistic missiles by providing immediate, flexible, and effective combat helicopter support anywhere, anytime, and on time. A normal response mission carries a pilot, copilot, flight engineer, and four Security Forces personnel. The flight engineer is the spotter, guiding the pilots during takeoff, hovering, landing, and cargo pickup. During Minot's flood of June 2011, the squadron provided 24-hour standby alert for search and rescue missions, distinguished visitor support, media transport, and logistics deliveries.

Due to security considerations, the author did not have access to the squadron's active operations. In August 2016, the author was given access to the 341st Missile Squadron on Malmstrom Air Force Base, Montana; photographs of this squadron are used here for similar Minot activities.

The Bell UH-1 Iroquois helicopter is used by the 54th Helicopter Squadron on Minot Air Force Base. It is an all-weather-capable aircraft, so winter weather is not an operational obstacle for search and rescue or medical evacuations. A wounded man on a stretcher is pictured being carried to a helicopter. (Courtesy Minot Air Force Base, 5th Bomb Wing Historian.)

Three UH-1Ns are lined up in a row on the 54th Helicopter Squadron's parking ramp on Minot Air Force Base. Rotors are secured in line with the fuselage at the rear of the helicopter to prevent damage from high winds. (Courtesy Minot Air Force Base, 5th Bomb Wing Historian.)

This UH-1N helicopter is on static display to the south side of the main entrance to Francis E. Warren Air Force Base in Cheyenne, Wyoming. The 90th Missile Wing uses UH-1Ns for missile site security and support. (Author's collection.)

On Minot Air Force Base, a UH-1N is pictured in the standard Air Force gray paint scheme inside a 91st Missile Wing vehicle security area. The helicopters are frequently used for transporting distinguished visitors and escorting Minuteman transporter-erectors. (Author's collection.)

The 54th Helicopter Squadron is equipped with seven UH-1Ns. The squadron has a modern maintenance and storage facility for its assigned helicopters. This is crucial for winter and inclement weather protection for these utility helicopters. (Author's collection.)

A 54th Helicopter Squadron helicopter is on the ready launch pad to respond to an alert from the 91st Missile Wing Command Post regarding an intrusion alarm at one of the wing's unmanned missile launch facilities. (Author's collection.)

A second 54th Helicopter Squadron UH-1N, with transport wheels attached to the helicopter's landing skids, has been pulled out of the hangar by a tow truck to a launch position. This one is in the green color used on Air Force Global Strike Command helicopters. (Author's collection.)

This incredible view is out of the right side of a 40th Helicopter Squadron UH-1N approaching 341st Missile Wing Missile Alert Facility Lima-01 at Malmstrom Air Force Base. (Courtesy Malmstrom Air Force Base, 341st Missile Wing Public Affairs.)

This is the left side of a UH-1N landed in the Malmstrom Air Force Base 341st Missile Wing Tactical Response Force training area to practice responding to a threatened missile launch facility. (Courtesy Malmstrom Air Force Base, 341st Missile Wing Public Affairs.)

Four tactical response force team members exit a UH-1N at Malmstrom Air Force Base. (Courtesy Malmstrom Air Force Base, 341st Missile Wing Public Affairs.)

When a 91st Missile Wing convoy leaves the Minot Air Force Base Weapons Storage Area, there are Security Forces vehicles in the lead in armored Humvees and other vehicles in the rear to protect the convoy. In the air, over the convoy, is a 54th Helicopter Squadron UH-1N carrying a four-person nuclear weapons attack team, the emergency backup and supplement to the ground Security Forces personnel. (Courtesy Minot Air Force Base, 91st Missile Wing Public Affairs.)

The Air Force is looking to replace its 72 UH-1Ns with either an existing or a new helicopter design. One of the front runners is the HH-60M Black Hawk. It has a longer range, higher speed, and greater payload. (Author's collection.)

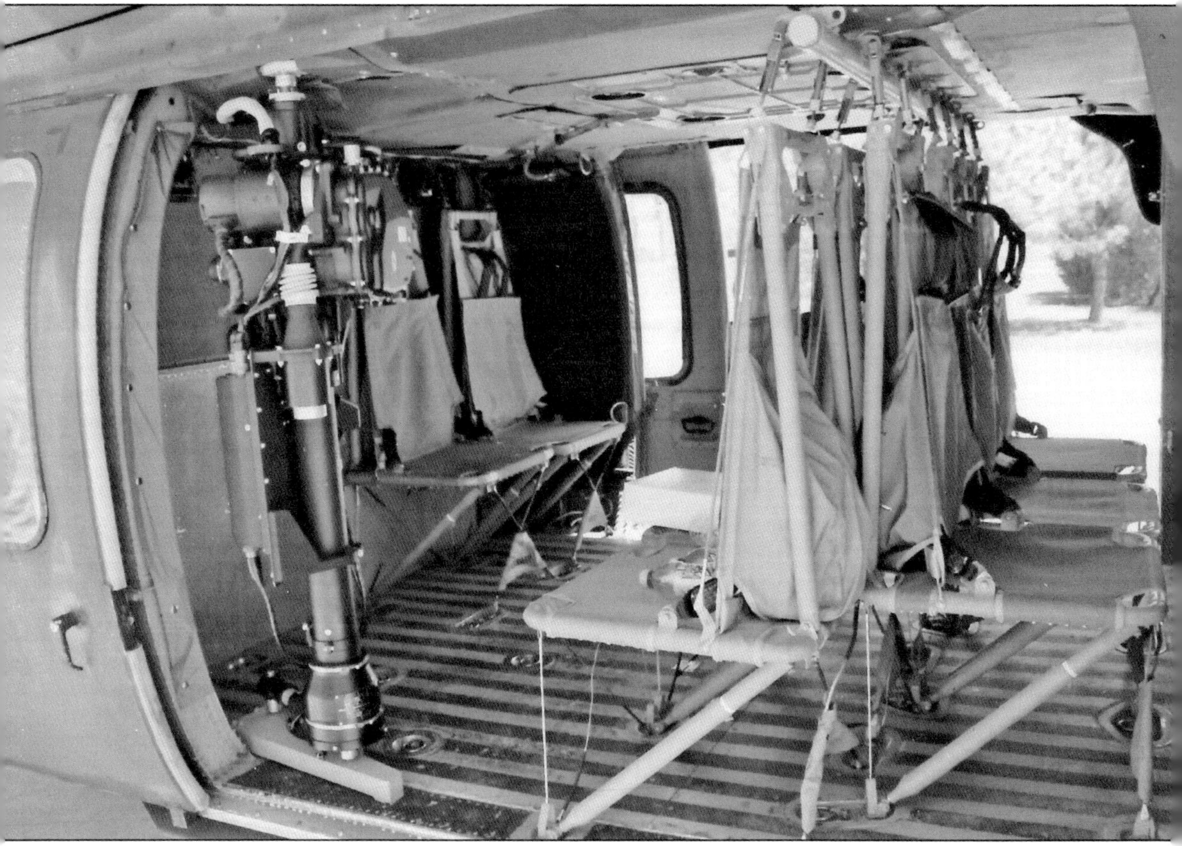

This interior view of the Black Hawk helicopter shows the larger crew and passenger capacity, which would provide improved operational capabilities for the 54th Helicopter Squadron. (Author's collection.)

Eight

91st Missile Wing 1961–Present

The strategic location of Minot Air Force Base, 75 miles from the geographic center of North America, is ideal for a Minuteman intercontinental ballistic missile base. Engineering test borings confirmed the topographic stability for subterranean construction.

In September 1961, a temporary construction headquarters was set up on Minot Air Force Base. The US Army Corps of Engineers served as the prime construction manager for Peter Kiewit & Sons Construction of Omaha, Nebraska. It built 15 missile alert facilities, including the site's underground launch command centers, 150 launch facilities (silos), and associated support facilities. Construction began in January 1962. At the peak of construction, there were 6,000 workers, 1,100 vehicles, and 115 cranes to meet the construction completion dates for the missile field and support facilities.

The 91st Missile Wing's mission is to defend the United States with safe, secure intercontinental ballistic missiles, ready to immediately put a nuclear warhead on target. The wing's missile field around Minot Air Force Base covers 8,500 square miles.

Even though the Minuteman III can carry three nuclear warheads, under the Strategic Arms Reduction Treaty, each missile can only be armed with one warhead. The Minuteman III has an expected end-of-life in 2030.

Even though the Minuteman III is an old weapon system, the Air Force is modernizing the system and its support functions. Periodically, to test the reliability of the Minuteman III, an operational missile's warhead is removed, and the missile is removed from its silo and transported to Vandenberg Air Force Base, California, for a reliability launch by a 91st Missile Wing combat crew, successfully impacting into the Kwajalein Atoll in the Pacific Ocean.

Due to security considerations, the author did not have access to the squadron's active operations. In August 2016, the author was given access to the 341st Missile Squadron on Malmstrom Air Force Base, including access to a missile alert facility and Security Forces operations; photographs taken then are used here to represent similar Minot activities. This provides an inside look at the nuclear deterrence of the United States by the Air Force Global Strike Command.

The 91st Missile Wing consists of the 640th, 741st, and 742nd Missile Squadrons; 91st Operations Support Squadron; and 54th Helicopter Squadron. Pictured is the 91st Missile Wing's headquarters building. (Author's collection.)

Launch facility construction started with earth scrapers digging a 12-foot-deep trench, deepened to 32 feet with backhoes. A drill crane finished the excavation to 84 feet. (Courtesy Malmstrom Air Force Base, 341st Missile Wing Historian.)

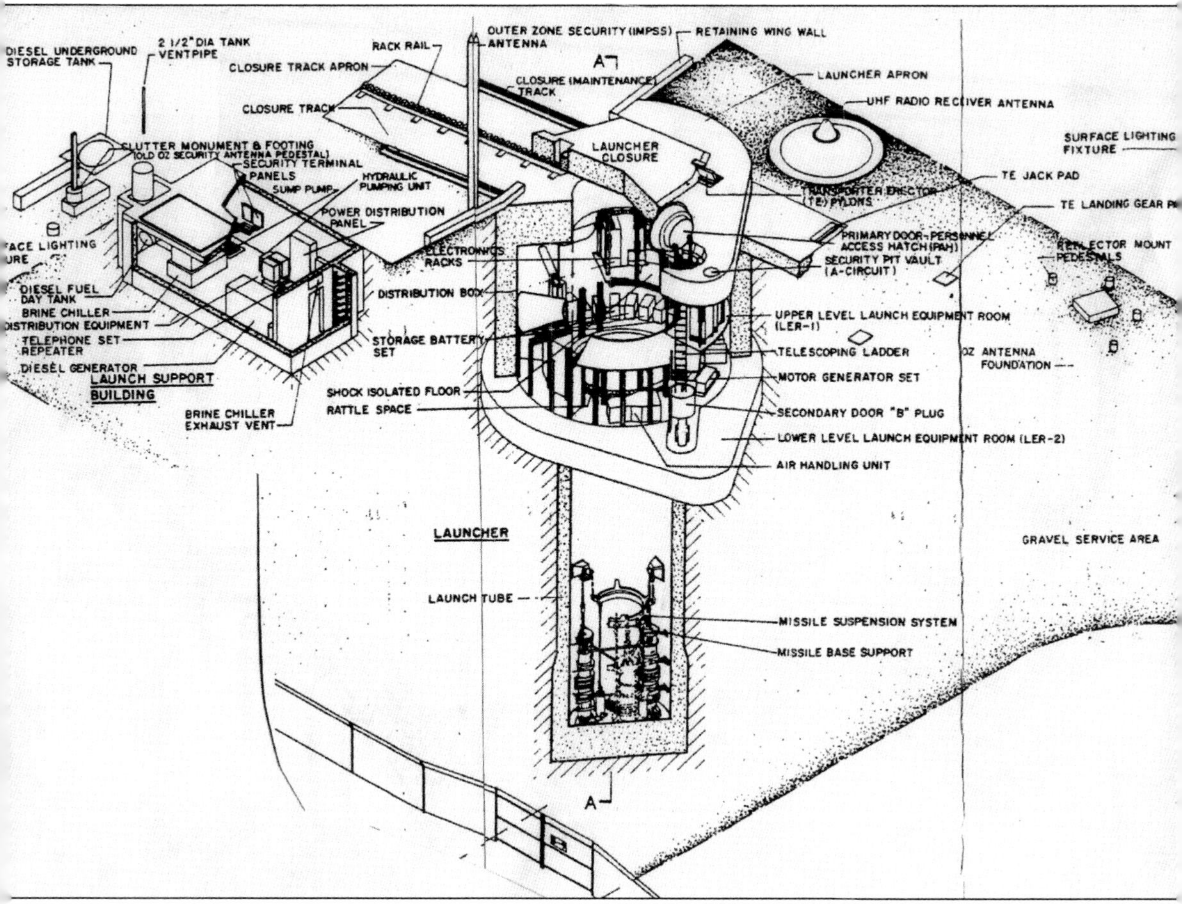

This drawing of a Minuteman III intercontinental ballistic missile silo shows its support facilities in the launch facility. The Minuteman silo appears simple from the ground, but there are extensive underground structures and equipment. (Courtesy Malmstrom Air Force Base, 341st Missile Wing Historian.)

Heavy-lift cranes lower a steel cylinder 12 feet in diameter into the completed excavation. (Courtesy Malmstrom Air Force Base, 341st Missile Wing Historian.)

Reinforced concrete was poured into a form around the steel cylinder and allowed to harden to a specific strength to withstand a nearby nuclear detonation. (Courtesy Malmstrom Air Force Base, 341st Missile Wing Historian.)

The top of the launch tube is covered with concrete and a steel blast closure door. The back of the closure door is pointed and sloped to clear debris from a nuclear attack or heavy snow as it rides on rails. (Courtesy Malmstrom Air Force Base, 341st Missile Wing Historian.)

Once construction work was completed on a Minuteman launch facility, it presented a clean profile at ground level, as at D-09, shown here, a former 44th Strategic Missile Wing facility on Ellsworth Air Force Base. The 91st Missile Wing's launch facilities had the same profile when completed. (Author's collection.)

The 91st Missile Wing Launch Facility Delta Flight (D-06) is adjacent to Highway 83 south of Minot. It is secured by a single chain-link fence, with a locked double vehicle access gate for the first level of site security. (Author's collection.)

North of Minot Air Force Base, adjacent to Highway 83, is Launch Facility Juliet (J-10). The sloped end of the launch closure door is visible, with security fencing, access gate, communication antennas, onsite remotely controlled monitors, and sensors. (Author's collection.)

What appears from a distance to be a wood utility pole at Launch Facility D-09, formerly of the 44th Strategic Missile Wing on Ellsworth Air Force Base, is actually part of the remotely controlled monitoring system for the launch facility. (Author's collection.)

This photograph, taken at Launch Facility India (I-02) by one of the remotely operated security cameras, indicates the high-quality image that can be obtained. It provides an elevated view of the interior of a launch facility. (Courtesy Minot Air Force Base, 91st Missile Wing Public Affairs.)

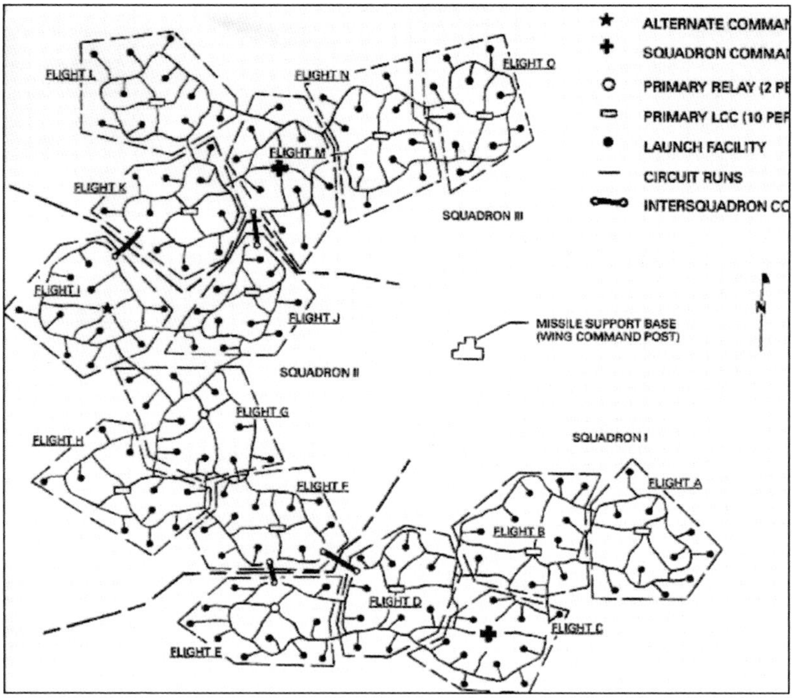

This image provides the general locations of Minot Air Force Base's 91st Missile Wing Minuteman facilities, 15 flights of 10 missiles each. This demonstrates the large area of the wing's missile field. (Courtesy Minot Air Force Base, 91st Missile Wing Public Affairs.)

In this photograph of Launch Facility Delta (D-05), the microwave communications dish antenna is aimed in the direction of its missile alert facility (D-01). Communications are sent to the underground launch control center. (Author's collection.)

Once completed, the excavations for the 150 launch facilities, 15 missile alert facilities, and underground launch control centers were backfilled with the removed dirt. (Courtesy Malmstrom Air Force Base, 341st Missile Wing Historian.)

The communication trench was filled with shielded cable coated with waterproofing material using a flatbed truck carrying a large cable roll. The trench was then backfilled, disappearing into surrounding land. (Courtesy Malmstrom Air Force Base, 341st Missile Wing Historian.)

This launch control center is 32 feet below the launch control support building. The steel shell is being assembled, with initial steel re-enforcing rebar being wrapped and welded in place and backfilled. (Courtesy Malmstrom Air Force Base, 341st Missile Wing Historian.)

Welding of steel rebar is nearly complete in this photograph for the launch control center and its launch control support building. The slanted steel tube is an emergency escape. (Courtesy Malmstrom Air Force Base, 341st Missile Wing Historian.)

In the foreground is a diesel fuel tank for the launch control support building's emergency power generators, encased in concrete. The smaller cylinder is for sewage overflow. (Courtesy Malmstrom Air Force Base, 341st Missile Wing Historian.)

Concrete has been poured into the access shaft, forming a base for the shaft's construction to the surface. Forms are being filled with concrete, and in the top third of the shaft, rebar work is in progress. (Courtesy Malmstrom Air Force Base, 341st Missile Wing Historian.)

Partial backfill covers the launch command center, launch control support building, and support equipment. Construction continues on the access shaft to the launch control support building. (Courtesy Malmstrom Air Force Base, 341st Missile Wing Historian.)

A freight elevator, at the top level, provides controlled access from the missile alert facility to the launch control support building below through the Security Forces section, which controls entrance to the underground capsule. This photograph was taken at the Ronald Reagan Minuteman Museum in North Dakota. (Author's collection.)

At the bottom of the access shaft, the freight elevator's steel curtain doors are open, showing the entrance into the tunnel junction. To the left is the launch control equipment building, and to the right is the launch command center. (Author's collection.)

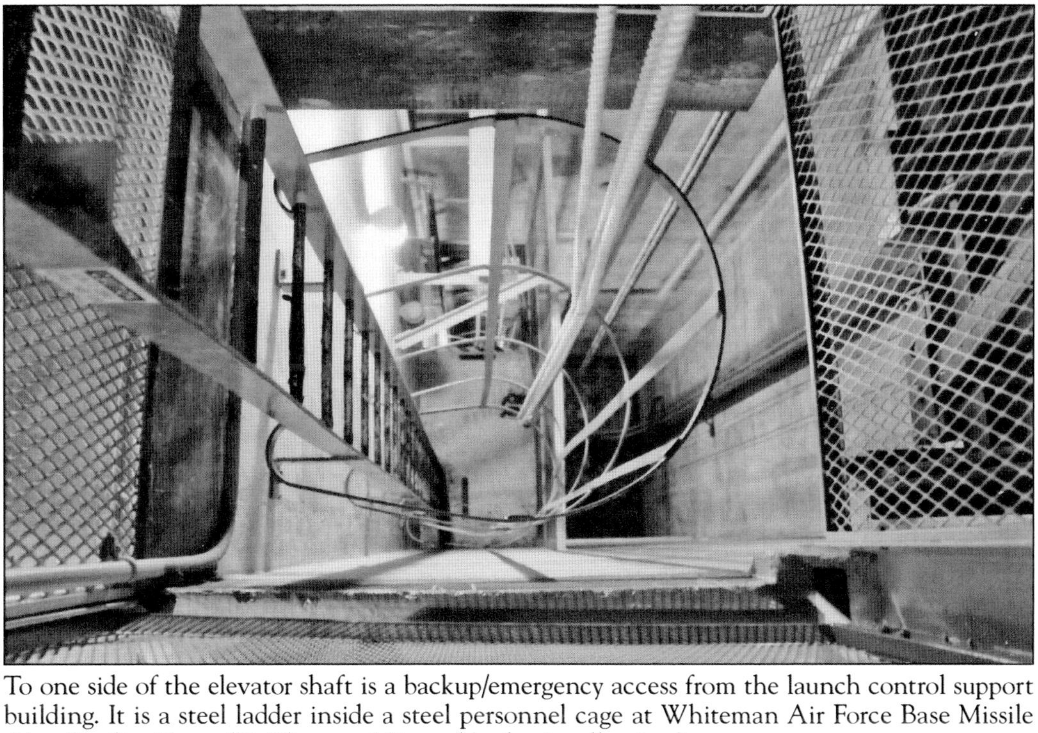

To one side of the elevator shaft is a backup/emergency access from the launch control support building. It is a steel ladder inside a steel personnel cage at Whiteman Air Force Base Missile Alert Facility Oscar (O-01), as on Minot. (Author's collection.)

At the end of the corridor from the freight elevator is the tunnel junction. The box contains equipment to cut into the launch control center during an emergency. This photograph was taken at the Ronald Reagan Minuteman Museum. (Author's collection.)

This photograph was taken looking down the connecting tunnel from the launch control equipment building. The thick interior concrete walls, rectangular in shape, mask the tubular shape of the pressure vessel's steel and concrete construction. (Author's collection.)

A heavy blast door, closed during alert operations, protects the launch control equipment building. The blast door can be opened or closed by authorized personnel with the correct tumbler lock combination. (Author's collection.)

Inside the launch control equipment building, commercial power is routed through electrical distribution equipment and replaced by emergency power generation equipment when under threat of imminent nuclear attack. (Author's collection.)

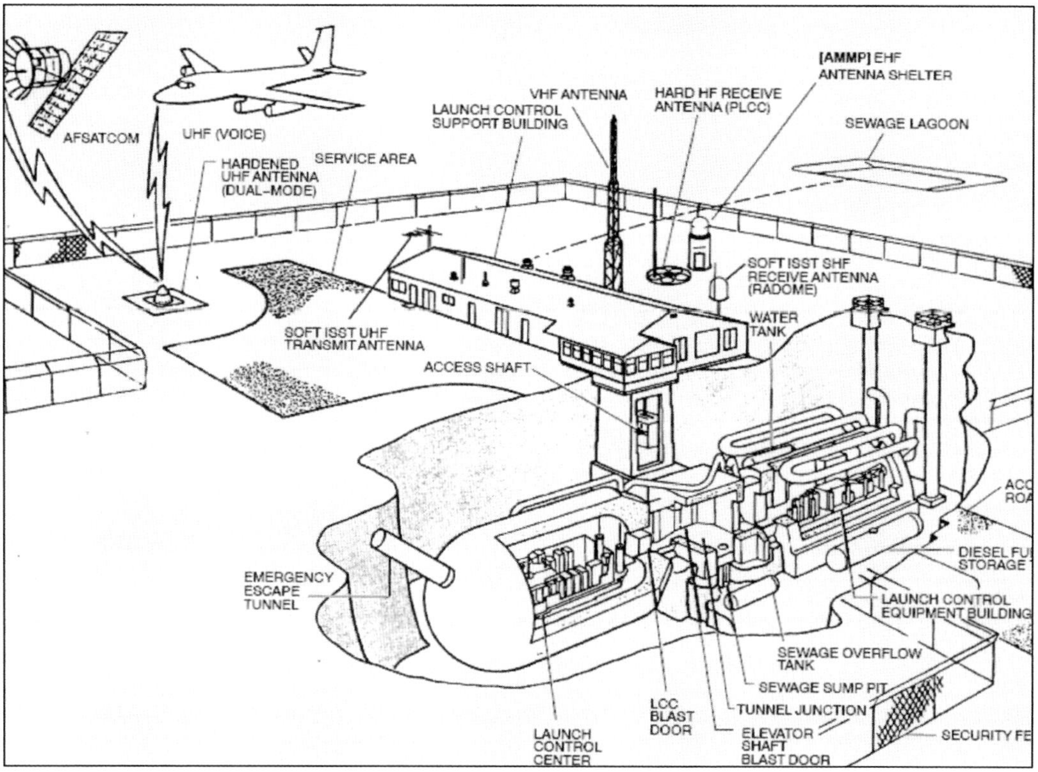

This layout of an Air Force Global Strike Command Minuteman missile alert facility is used in the 15 facilities in Minot Air Force Base's large missile field. (Courtesy Minot Air Force Base, 5th Bomb Wing Public Affairs.)

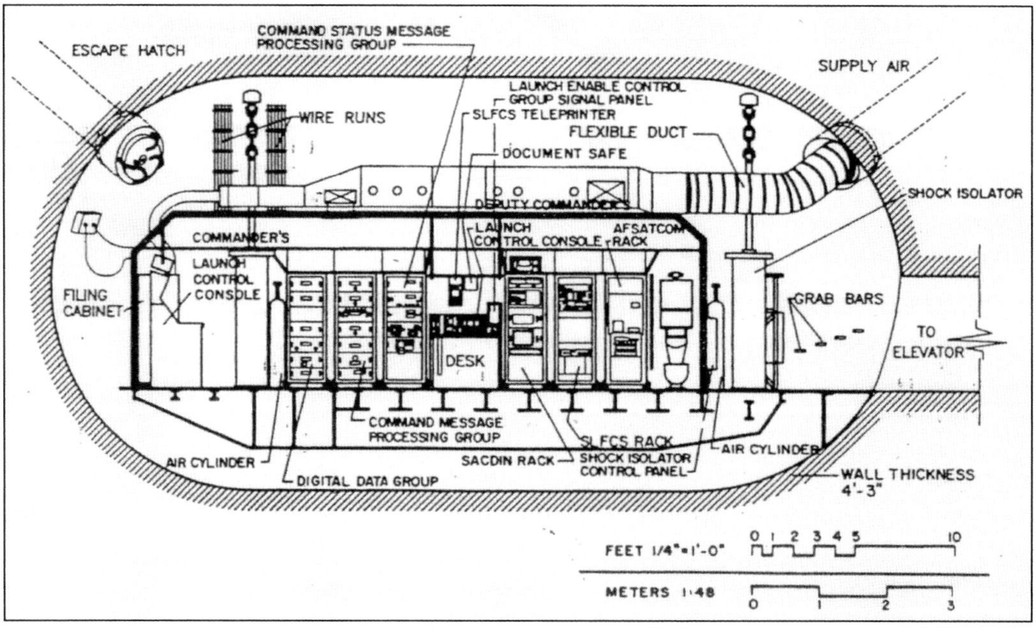

The right-side interior of a launch control center is shown, with the various equipment used by the on-duty missile launch officers. (Courtesy Minot Air Force Base, 5th Bomb Wing Public Affairs.)

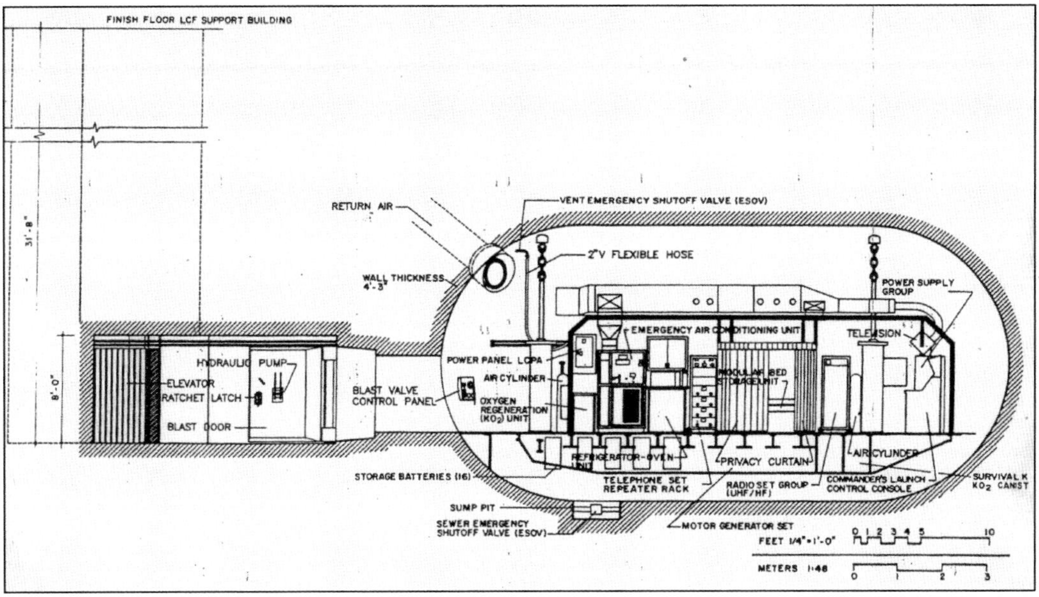

The left-side interior of a launch control center is shown, with the various equipment used by the on-duty missile launch officers. (Courtesy Minot Air Force Base, 5th Bomb Wing Public Affairs.)

This launch control center is similar to the 15 used on Minot. This is Missile Launch Facility Alpha (A-01) on Malmstrom Air Force Base, pictured on July 15, 2014. In front is 2nd Lt. Wesley Griffith, and at rear is 1st Lt. Kalie Grimley. (Courtesy Minot Air Force Base, 5th Bomb Wing Public Affairs.)

A heavy and thick launch control center blast door is being pushed open by a missile launch officer on duty. The door is designed to protect from a nuclear attack. (Courtesy Malmstrom Air Force Base, 341st Missile Wing Public Affairs.)

This access gate leads to Missile Launch Facility Lima (L-01) at Malmstrom Air Force Base, similar to the facilities on Minot. The white tanks are for refueling vehicles driven to the facility. (Courtesy Malmstrom Air Force Base, 341st Missile Wing Public Affairs.)

This side view shows the main entrance of L-01 Launch Control Support Building. It looks like a standard one-story ranch-style building of wood frame construction, not hardened. (Courtesy Malmstrom Air Force Base, 341st Missile Wing Public Affairs.)

A Minuteman transporter-erector is pictured on Minot Air Force Base. The vehicle provides secure and enclosed transportation of a Minuteman missile to and from a launch facility as required for replacement and maintenance. (Author's collection.)

This Minuteman III intercontinental ballistic missile is on static display at Malmstrom Air Force Base in Montana. (Author's collection.)

A Minuteman transporter-erector, in 90-degree vertical position, lowers a Minuteman missile into a silo at a launch facility. (Courtesy Malmstrom Air Force Base, 341st Missile Wing Public Affairs.)

Sr. Amn. Dereck Baker, 341st Missile Maintenance Squadron handling technician, lowers a Minuteman III solid-propellant replacement booster into Launch Facility Echo (E-08) on August 18, 2009; the same procedure is used at Minot. (Courtesy Malmstrom Air Force Base, 341st Missile Wing Public Affairs.)

A Minuteman III intercontinental ballistic missile is pictured inside its silo. The hardened underground launcher serves as a controlled-temperature, long-term protective storage enclosure and launcher. (Courtesy Malmstrom Air Force Base, 341st Missile Wing Public Affairs.)

On May 24, 2016, an Air Force Global Strike Command missile officer launch crew pre-departure briefing is held for 15 crews on Malmstrom Air Force Base. Similar briefings are held on Minot. (Courtesy Malmstrom Air Force Base, 341st Missile Wing Public Affairs.)

Missile alert crews on Minot Air Force Base (like those on other missile bases) drive to their assigned missile alert facility to change out the on-duty launch control center crews. They drive from their base in white, unmarked crew cab trucks. (Author's collection.)

The author was flown by helicopter to Missile Alert Facility Lima-01 for a briefing on the functions in the launch control center; such briefings occur daily on Minot Air Force Base. (Courtesy Malmstrom Air Force Base, 341st Missile Wing Public Affairs.)

The author receives a facilities briefing in L-01's launch control support building, similar in appearance to those on Minot Air Force Base. (Courtesy Malmstrom Air Force Base, 341st Missile Wing Public Affairs.)

The author received a Security Forces briefing in the security control room before going underground into the launch control center for a briefing on the functions of the center. (Courtesy Malmstrom Air Force Base, 341st Missile Wing Public Affairs.)

Pictured is the L-01 dining room, with the kitchen to the left. (Courtesy Malmstrom Air Force Base, 341st Missile Wing Public Affairs.)

Part of the facility upgrade program completed in 2016 was stainless-steel food preparation and storage in the kitchen. (Courtesy Malmstrom Air Force Base, 341st Missile Wing Public Affairs.)

An L-01 facility chef prepares a food order for onsite personnel and visitors, maintenance personnel, or additional Security Forces during missile change-outs or maintenance. (Courtesy Malmstrom Air Force Base, 341st Missile Wing Public Affairs.)

A requested upgrade to a missile alert facility was the installation of exercise equipment for onsite physical fitness. (Courtesy Malmstrom Air Force Base, 341st Missile Wing Public Affairs.)

Pictured is the L-01 sleeping area for onsite shift personnel or visitors. (Courtesy Malmstrom Air Force Base, 341st Missile Wing Public Affairs.)

Bibliography

A Brief History of the 5th Bomb Wing. Minot, ND: Minot Air Force Base, 5th Bomb Wing Public Affairs, 1992.

A Fortieth Anniversary History of Minot Air Force Base, Minot, North Dakota. Minot, ND: Minot Air Force Base, 5th Bomb Wing Public Affairs, 2008.

Air Force Pilots Remember U-2 Spy Plane Flights from Minot Air Force Base. Minot, ND: Minot Air Force Base, 5th Bomb Wing Public Affairs, 2002.

B-52H Stratofortress on Minot Air Force Base. Minot, ND: Minot Air Force Base, 5th Bomb Wing Public Affairs, 2013.

54th Helicopter Squadron. Minot, ND: Minot Air Force Base, 91st Missile Wing Public Affairs, 2013.

"5th Bomb Wing." *US Air Force Fact Sheet.* Minot, ND: Minot Air Force Base, 5th Bomb Wing Public Affairs, 1986.

History of Minot Air Force Base, 1980. Minot, ND: Minot Air Force Base, 5th Bomb Wing Public Affairs, 1980.

Minot Air Force Base. Minot, ND: Minot Air Force Base, 5th Bomb Wing Public Affairs, 2001.

Minot Air Force Base History. Minot, ND: Minot Air Force Base, 5th Bomb Wing Public Affairs, 2013.

Minuteman at Minot Air Force Base. Minot, ND: Minot Air Force Base, 91st Missile Wing Public Affairs, 2013.

91st Missile Wing (Rough Riders). Minot, ND: Minot Air Force Base, 91st Missile Wing Public Affairs, 2013.

The Wonders of a B-52. Minot, ND: Minot Air Force Base, 5th Bomb Wing Public Affairs, 2015.

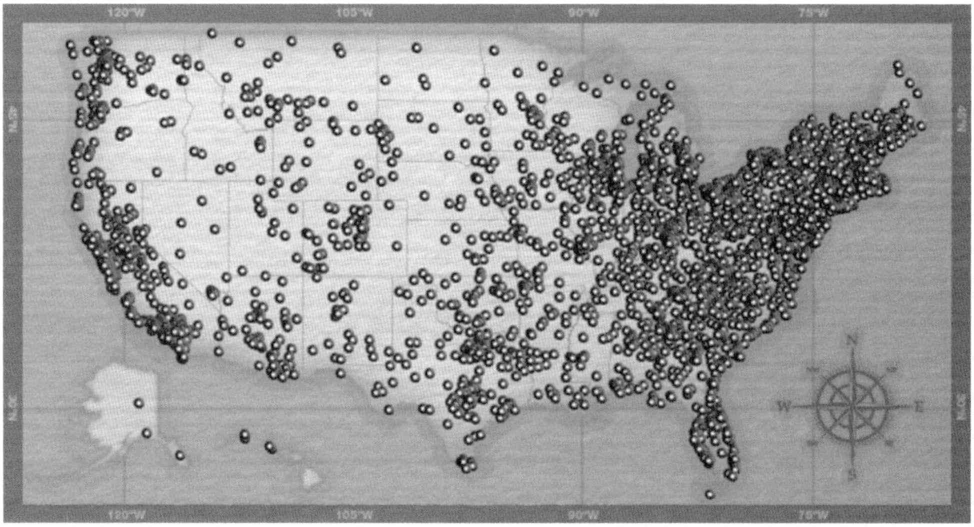